VETERAN AND VINTAGE CARS

VETERAN AND VINTAGE CARS

VETERAN AND VINTAGE CARS

PETER ROBERTS

PAUL HAMLYN
LONDON · NEW YORK · SYDNEY · TORONTO

contents

Published by
THE HAMLYN PUBLISHING GROUP LTD
LONDON · NEW YORK · SYDNEY · TORONTO
Hamlyn House, The Centre, Feltham, Middlesex
© Copyright 1963 The Hamlyn Publishing Group Ltd
First published 1963 Seventh impression 1970
Printed in Czechoslovakia by TSNP, Martin

in the beginning . . .

Barely three generations have passed since the motor car first appeared on the highways of the world. Just over sixty years ago the petrol engine shakily and noisily announced its arrival on the British scene. It was an unwelcome arrival. Unwelcome, that is, to all save a few far-sighted pioneers, men who realised that the transport of people and goods at the end of the nineteenth century was appallingly inefficient, falling far behind the advances of science in the fields of production and industrial mechanisation.

The business of using the common roads for fast, long distance travelling had in fact been the preoccupation of a number of men since the latter part of the eighteenth century, but it had been an exhausting battle against the heaviest of political odds.

The public and the legislators were for many years reluctant to allow mechanical transport on the roads on three main counts. The noise frightened their horses, the vehicles were held to be largely uncontrollable (which they were), and the enormous clouds of dust they drew from the unmetalled roads of the day were, to say the least, inconvenient. These arguments were valid until well into the first decade of the twentieth century . . .

The earliest mechanical motive power was steam. Even as far back as the Ancient Greeks the principles and the mechanics of the steam turbine were known, and a working model turbine had been made, but it is still surprising to learn that a moderately successful steam coach could be seen in operation as early as 1769. Designed and built by a Frenchman, Joseph Cugnot, it literally blazed its trail through the streets of Paris long before the advent of the railways, and more than twenty years before the first steam-boat was considered to be a practical commercial proposition. It was, however, alone in its brief

Cugnot's steam-driven vehicle.

An 18th-century steam coach in Britain.

5

Hancock's 'Enterprise' steam carriage of 1833.

success. Enormously heavy and expensive to run (compared with horse-drawn vehicles) it sowed a harvest of panic and horror as it clanked its dinosaur way about the roads at a full two miles an hour.

Several other intrepid designers brought out steam coaches during the first three decades of the nineteenth century. They, too, had a rough time. In company with railed locomotive projects of that time, they suffered strong opposition. Horse-coach companies managed, through Acts of Parliament, to increase the turnpike tariffs, sometimes to ten times those paid by horse-drawn vehicles. Other less constitutional methods were also used to force them off the roads, even to the setting up of barricades.

Nevertheless, some of these enterprises were successful, and here and there regular short services of steam coaches were inaugurated. The great weight and bulk of mechanical transport at this stage precluded the building of small private machines, and channelled designers into producing passenger-carrying commercial vehicles.

As the railways overcame their own peculiar problems and secured a foothold as the only mass means of long-distance travel, so road transport began, if not to die, to receive several body-blows to its advancement. The steam-carriage cult waned.

Gurney's steam coach, which carried travellers between London and Bath in the 1830s.

Fourteen miles an hour at threepence a mile is the claim for this coach of the mid-nineteenth century.

Its renaissance occurred in the 1860s, by which time engine sizes had been whittled down somewhat, and smaller, more manoeuvreable vehicles could be built. Also, the turnpike system was dying, allowing less expensive travel from place to place.

A few years later new names began to make news, names such as the Comte de Dion, Daimler, Bollée (who in 1875 made a marathon run of 142 miles in his steam car) and Serpollet, who had also begun to experiment with road vehicles.

During these years several new Acts had been passed, Acts that set up a scale of speeds, stated that vehicles should be conducted by two drivers, and so on; all made, one feels, for the express purpose of discouragement.

In 1865 came the now infamous 'Red Flag' Act, which stepped up the number of necessary drivers to three, reduced the maximum speed to four miles an hour in the country and two through a town, and enforced a vehicle to be preceded by a footman bearing a red flag.

Thirteen years later the red flag was no longer law – but the foot-man and the speed limits were. Until 1896 road vehicles (most of which by this date could have moved quite rapidly) were for amuse-ment only – a method of travelling at less than a fast walking pace with only the added virtue of keeping one's feet dry.

Meanwhile, on the Continent, no such stifling restrictions held back the progress of road transport. Gottlieb Daimler had invented his petrol engine and Karl Benz had built his first car. Messieurs

Steam wagonette, 1868.

Panhard and Levassor had designed and run a road vehicle using Daimler's engine as its power unit. Britain lagged fearfully behind both Europe and America in the development of the oil-burning engine; the few who had gone ahead with designing and building road transport had unbelievable hurdles to overcome. The licensing law was just one of the early obstacles; local authorities were empowered to exact a fee of £10, which permitted a vehicle to be used on roads *only within the county boundaries*. An expedition to a neighbouring shire could bring down another £10 fee on the head of an unfortunate traveller.

It was largely due to crippling laws of this kind that what is generally regarded as the first genuine British car did not appear until 1895. America, at this time, was forging ahead with White steam cars, Stanley's elegant steamers, and Henry Ford had almost completed his first vehicle.

In France (while we in Britain still had our footman) the first motor race was being organised. In 1894, after a series of competition trials, the famous Paris to Rouen race was held. It is, perhaps, some indication of the attitude of the Continentals to the new automobilism to record that this race was won—by a de Dion steam vehicle—at an average speed of 12 m.p.h., a feat that would have cost a fortune in fines in England!

During the last years of the Victorian century there were those in England who, although bound hand and foot in the use of cars on the roads, agitated hotly for the repeal of acts which appeared to be designed to prevent a motor industry being born. In 1896, continued and vigorous representation led to the great charter for motorists, the amendments in the Locomotives on Highways Act.

The story of motoring—in Britain at least—has been the story of the struggle by the bold few for the advancement of road transport. Since it all began back in 1769, it has been a long, hard battle; a fight against prejudice, a fight against conflicting interests, a fight against resistance to change. In many ways it still is . . .

The Benz Motorwagen of 1888.

Benz Patent Motorwagen, 1886.

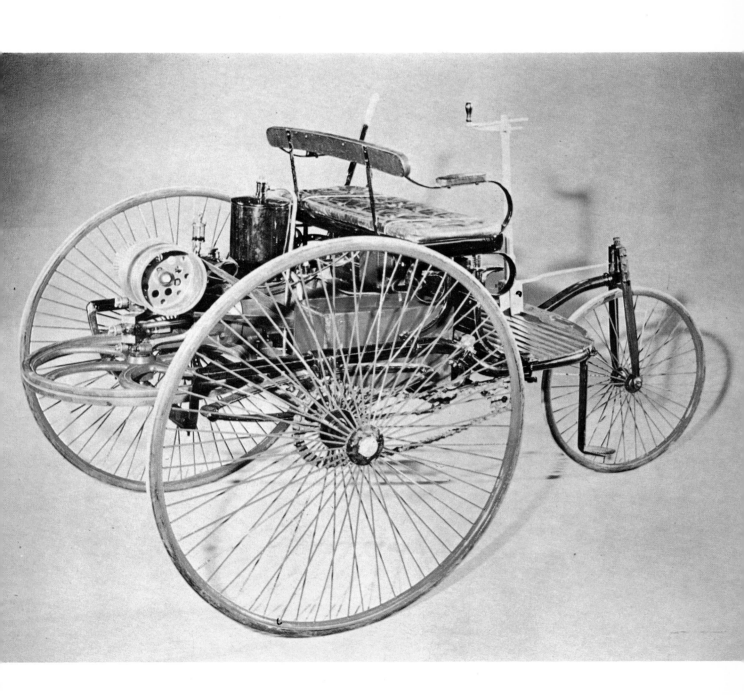

Daimler's 1886 car.

Mercedes Simplex Tourer, 1902.

Mercedes sports car, 1924.

device of the devil?

Horses pulling a tram along Cardiff's St Mary's Street plunged and kicked when they saw it. Faces peered through windows at it. Pedestrians came to a halt, the genteel pretending indifference to it, the less self-conscious gazing open-mouthed at it.

A policeman who came to break up the gathering crowd stopped and gaped at it with them.

This was the scene, according to a contemporary magazine account, when in 1897 the first car came to South Wales.

However, the reputedly volatile Welsh seem to have been quite phlegmatic about the horseless carriage's arrival compared to people in other parts of Britain.

Drivers told of country-folk fleeing at their approach in some places. A motorist who booked into a big Hastings hotel in 1899 complained that he was ordered to leave again when he told them that he had brought his motor car with him.

The management were certain it would explode or burst into flames!

In London, pioneer motorists were forced to run the gauntlet of jeers and shouts from the drivers of hansom cabs and omnibuses, whose horses were frequently frightened by the noisy newcomers to the roads.

In this connection, Mr. H. J. Mulliner of the famous coach-building family, a founder member of the R.A.C., recalls driving a 3 h.p. de Dion across Waterloo Bridge in 1899, just as a detachment of cavalry were crossing on their way to the Boer War.

The smoking, snorting de Dion struck more fear into the cavalry than ever the Boers could have done, and the superbly smart, disciplined ranks became a chaotic rabble in seconds. Mr. Mulliner, whose engine chose this moment to stop, was surrounded—and berated—by crimson-faced officers.

A few horsemen of that time were far-seeing enough to approach motorists with the request that they might be allowed to lead their

A de Dion Voiturette sweeps past the crowds during the 1,000 Miles Trial.

The cars taking part in the 1,000 Miles Trial of 1900 assemble in the Agricultural Hall, London.

A rest outside Edinburgh for the drivers of the 1900 marathon.

horses up to the automobiles and accustom them to the sound and smell. But to most, motoring was just 'the new French sporting craze'. Some attacked it and (presiently, it must be admitted) forecast accidents and fatalities.

Some mocked it. Cartoonists ridiculed the goggles and the big, furry Eskimo style coats.

Life was trying enough for the Victorian motorist without this hostility and derision. Because garages were almost unknown and the only help likely to be available in a breakdown was a blacksmith's, he had to understand his car and also to equip himself with spares and tools down to a collapsible bucket for fetching water, and a hatchet to cut staves for levering his car out of muddy ruts.

He had to check his petrol carefully, for stockists were hard to find. A list published in the *Autocar* for those intending to tour at Easter 1899 named only four in London and 29 elsewhere, including a village chemist and a grocer.

The wise motorist also took with him—no matter how short his journey was intended to be—a box of biscuits, a bottle of wine and a packed overnight bag in case a major breakdown meant a delay of hours.

Starting the car could be a long-drawn-out performance. Throttle and mixture controls had to be set after consideration of the weather, and the engine turned over manually—revolving the flywheel when no starting handle was fitted.

The carburettor had to be filled, and it was not unknown for petrol to have to be injected into the cylinder with a syringe.

14

Even after the engine had been swung into clattering life, the ignition advanced, and the car driven off, the driver had such essential duties to perform as checking the drip-feed lubrication.

Sometimes the only way of climbing a steep hill would be to get out and push. On other occasions it was possible to climb a hill backwards, making use of the reverse gear's lower ratio. The car would often begin to run backwards down a hill, despite the iron sprag or 'devil drag' which could be lowered to dig into the road to prevent this hair-raising occurrence.

To keep warm in inclement weather was extremely difficult. Sheets of brown paper worn beneath the coat helped, but the only completely snug protection was a thick rug wrapped around the legs and this, though excellent for passengers, tended to hamper the driver.

Certainly the top hats and morning clothes demanded of men, and the elegant hats, dresses and gloves chosen by women on important occasions such as the Automobile Club runs were as unsuitable and impractical as could be imagined for wearing in open, breakdown-prone vehicles.

The Victorian motorist had also, of course, to contend with the disapproval of the law. The *Autocar* reported a case in 1899 in which a man named Jeal was convicted at Brighton of driving a motor car at a speed greater than was reasonable and proper, having regard to the traffic. He was fined £3 and costs or 21 days in jail, time to pay being refused.

His speed, according to the Chief Constable, was 12 m.p.h.

The *Autocar* report goes on, 'The defendant then asked the pace at which he was allowed to go . . . The magistrates' clerk said that if a motor car was used in Brighton he should think four m.p.h. would be fast enough for anybody'.

A dreaded 'sideslip' causes this competitor in the 1,000 Miles event to make unwelcome contact with a stone wall.

Motorists were to continue to find themselves in trouble with the police but the attitude of the general public to motoring underwent a change after the 1,000 mile Automobile Club trial of 1900.

The 65 competing cars swept through Bristol, Birmingham, Manchester, Carlisle, Edinburgh, Newcastle, Leeds, Sheffield, Nottingham and back to London. In their 18 days on the roads they had given many country people their first glimpse of a car.

And the public took to the car at last. Excited by the cars chasing each other through their towns they cheered the drivers and encouraged them to defy the 12 m.p.h. speed limit.

Many years later the organiser of the Trial, Claude Johnson, wrote: 'I am inclined to believe 100 years hence the 1,000 miles trial of 1900 will be looked upon as the event which first conclusively proved to the people of the United Kingdom that the automobile was not a freak but a vehicle which had to be considered seriously.

'The manufacturers of motor cars engaged in the industry at the time admit that it was from that date that the public generally—apart from the unenlightened few—began to order motor cars in considerable numbers'.

As the car passed from the Victorian age to the Edwardian, the jeers died, the hatred of mechanical transport waned, and the country began to realise that the new form of travel was here to stay.

For twelve years this 1888 three-wheeler was forced to travel preceded by a footman. This photograph was taken at a London-Brighton Run.

The first full year of 'legalised' motoring was in 1897, when this Benz Dogcart was made.

laws of the land

The state of the highways of Britain and the numbers of vehicles that passed upon them began to concern authorities both national and local early in the 19th century. Until then most of our roads had been the property of landowners, property to leave in its original muddy, pot-holed condition or to improve as they saw fit.

In the Books of Statutes one can find the first glimmering of responsibility on the part of the state. Many curious Acts were passed in order to get work done on the roads, wordy pieces of legislation designed in many cases merely to get a dozen miles of narrow lane into passable order. One such Act, written into the book during the year 1813, states that it is an *Act passed in the fifty-third year of the reign of King George the Third for the repairing of the road from the City of Coventry to the Rugby Turnpike road in the Parish of Wolvey in the County of Warwick.* Today it seems rather like using a sledgehammer to kill an ant—but at least it was a beginning!

In 1861, just over a century ago, the government awoke to the fact that mechanically propelled vehicles—steam carriages—were increasing in numbers, and were a possible source of revenue. In August of that year an *Act to Regulate the use of Locomotives on Highways* begins: *Whereas the use of locomotives is likely to become common on turnpike and other roads . . . be it therefore enacted: For every locomotive propelled by its own power, containing within itself the machinery for its own propulsion . . .* and continues to list the fees for using toll roads. Every two tons of vehicle, it reads, were as one horse and waggon. Weight and sizes over certain limits were dealt with more severely.

Speeds of mechanical vehicles were limited to ten miles an hour in the countryside and five through a town or village. The fine for exceeding the limit, by the way, was £5—stiff even by today's standards. A more familiar feature of this Act was the stipulation that *The person in charge of the locomotive shall provide two efficient lights one on each side of same between the hours of one hour after sunset and one hour before sunrise.* Fine for failure to comply: £5.

Then in 1865 they really cracked down. An Act for *further regulating the use of locomotives on turnpike or other roads for agricultural and other purposes* laid down that: *Firstly at least three persons shall be employed to drive or conduct such a locomotive . . . Secondly that one of such persons, while any locomotive is in motion, shall precede such locomotive on foot by not less than sixty yards, and shall carry a red flag constantly displayed, and shall warn riders and drivers of horses of the approach of such locomotives and shall signal the driver thereof when it shall be necessary to stop . . . Fifthly every such locomotive shall be stopped by any person with a horse or carriage drawn by a horse putting up his hand.* This was the Act that also reduced the maximum speed to four miles an hour through the country and two through towns and villages.

As one may imagine, this Act brought the mechanical transport of the day more or less to a grinding halt.

Built for speed. In 1903 the legal limit was raised to 20 miles an hour.

The Highways and Locomotive (Amendment) Act of 1878 merely confused issues by laying down pettifogging regulations relating to tyre widths, weights, permissible hours of travelling, and a curious little rule stating that a mechanical vehicle should *consume its own smoke.*

The great charter of 1896 lies in the Statute Book coyly between a Judicial Trustee Act and a lengthy Lands and Heritage law.

It begins its stylised but momentous prose by calling itself *An Act to amend the law with respect to the use of Locomotives on Highways.* Thence to the Act itself commencing (as do all Acts) with these grandiose terms:

Be it enacted by the Queen's most excellent Majesty, by and with the advice of the Lords Spiritual and Temporal, and Commons, in this present Parliament assembled, and by the authority of the same, as follows :-

It goes on to repeal some of the restrictions on 'Light Locomotives', talks about lights, and states that a bell or other instrument must be affixed to all vehicles. Then, some way down the page, in paragraph 4, it says, in its negative way, that: *No light locomotive shall travel along a public highway at a greater speed than fourteen miles an hour.* The shackles were off!

Tradition has it that the 1896 Act permitted a motorist to drive without showing the red flag: this is not true. An Act of 1878 did in fact state that the flag was no longer necessary, but since it did not permit the use of a vehicle without a footman preceding it, there was not much to be gained at the time.

The Act of 1903 makes a modern reading in some of its parts. It has reference to driving a motor car on a public highway 'recklessly or negligently' and discourses long and thoroughly on the ways in which motorists may be penalised. It lays down the procedure for accidents, and cautions drivers not to forge their own licences.

In Section 9 it quietly gives the go-ahead to would-be suicides by repealing the Principal Act and stating that: . . . *but a person shall not, under any circumstances, drive a motor car on the public highway at a speed exceeding twenty miles an hour.*

Motoring, it seemed, had come to stay.

**bold
front**

Rolls-Royce, 1912.

Radiators wide and solid, or round as a locomotive boiler; all, except the unconventional Renault, had one characteristic in common. Their straight up-and-down, uncompromising lines. They presented a pugnacious front to the weather, no quarter given to lessening wind resistance. And very fine and upright these pre-aerodynamic aristocrats were . . .

Austin, 1912.

A four-cylinder 20/30 h.p. tourer.

Renault one-cylinder 4½ h.p. tonneau, 1901.

Hotchkiss, 1910.

Wolseley-Siddeley, 1909; four-cylinders, 14 h.p.

Gardner-Serpollet steamer, 1904.

De Dion Bouton 8 h.p. tourer, 1907.

cars
and kings

Royalty and the famous were among the first to make regular use of the motor car . . .

King George V (as Duke of York) aboard a 12 h.p. Panhard in 1900. The driver is the Hon. C. S. Rolls.

King Edward VII at Highcliffe Castle. The car is a 12 h.p. Daimler; the date, 1899.

Mark Twain . . .

. . . and Marie Lloyd.

A 1905 Daimler 'detachable' Limousine.

A 5 litre Cannstatt-Daimler of 1899.

the fathers of the motor car

No single man can rightly be called the inventor of the motor car; it was the product of many minds.

Two men, however, are generally regarded as the fathers of our modern mechanical transport: Karl Benz and Gottlieb Daimler. Benz, born in Mannheim, Germany, in 1844, designed and made the first petrol-driven horseless carriages to be produced commercially, and Daimler, a fellow countryman, born ten years before Benz, was the originator of the unit from which our modern engines are derived . . .

First of the line. The Benz three-wheeler of 1886.

Karl Benz was the son of one of the first locomotive drivers, and like his father, his bent was for mechanical science rather than the arts.

At his local school he became interested in photography (then in its infancy), in chemistry, and in clockwork motors, 'learning to feel the marvellous language that gear wheels talk when they mesh with one another', as he says in his autobiography.

When Benz was sixteen he entered the Karlsruhe Polytechnic; this proved to be the turning point of his life, directing his interests to 'a unit that could supplant the steam engine'.

When the young Karl had completed his courses he found a lowly job in the Karlsruhe Engineering Works. After a time it proved to be a dead-end post and he left.

History might have been otherwise if he had not left at that moment in time. He might never have succeeded in his later work; he might never even have taken it up. Or he might have produced his cars considerably earlier, for, by an odd chance, Gottlieb Daimler took over as senior engineer soon after Benz left. They had almost made contact.

In 1871 Benz went into business on his own. He opened what he called a 'factory for tin-working machinery', only to begin foundering in financial difficulties brought about by a stock market crash.

But Benz was used to lack of money—he had been raised in poverty

Karl Benz.

23

1888. More seats, but still three wheels.

—and had the necessary drive to combat it. He borrowed, founded a new business, designed a stationary engine, and began producing.

These first engines, some of them still workable today, carried his name around the world. His business prospered, he expanded, and persuaded his investors to allow him to devote some of his time to his first love, a mechanically propelled vehicle employing power more efficient than steam.

He chose as his 'shell' a light carriage with bicycle type rubber tyred wheels. In place of the shafts he put a third (steering) wheel. The small, four-cycle engine was built under the seat. A curious footnote to this is the fact that Benz made this first unit to incorporate a horizontal flywheel—he thought that a vertical one would prevent steering by its gyroscopic action!

In July 1886 an announcement in the local paper, the *Neue Badische Landeszeitung* read: 'A velocipede driven by Ligroin gas, built by the Reinische Gasmotorenfabrik of Benz & Cie. . . . was tested early this morning on the Ringstrasse, during which it operated satisfactorily.' Little enough to say about the event that heralded a new era.

The first long distance test, however, came as a surprise, even to Karl Benz himself. Aided by their mother, his two sons, Eugen and Richard, borrowed the machine while their father was still asleep one

The Benz 'Viktoria', 1893.

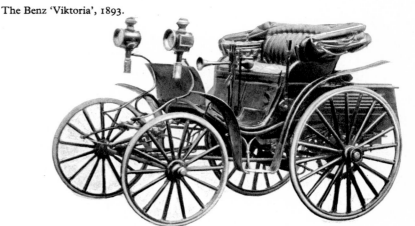

'Dos-à-Dos' by Benz, 1897.

morning, and took it for an unofficial joy-ride. They drove it the amazing distance of 70 miles—from Mannheim to Pforzheim—and back again. Despite rough roads, darkness, steep gradients, and several small breakdowns the boys, aged fifteen and thirteen, managed the trip without any major mishaps, performing all the roadside repairs themselves.

The boys—and their father—learned two useful lessons from this escapade. Firstly, it proved beyond doubt that the car was a practical proposition; and secondly, that it needed an extra low gear to negotiate the gradients.

Success in this project encouraged Benz to turn to the development of a four-wheeled car, and by 1893 he had built his first car 'with a steering mechanism with steering circles set on a tangent to the wheels'. He called this car the 'Viktoria', not after the English Queen of that name as is often thought, but to celebrate his victory over the complex steering problem.

The 'Velo'.

Model after improved model followed from the Benz factory. Styles were varied to suit diverse purposes. The Dos-à-Dos, The Brake, the Duc, the Mylord, the Ideal—greatly sought after in England— and many other types poured out of his Mannheim works, until by 1899 he was producing nearly 600 cars a year.

Meanwhile, Daimler had also been manufacturing motor cars . . .

Gottlieb Daimler was forced by his father into a classical education. But Latin was less attractive to him than practical, plane and solid

'Ideal', 1899.

Gottlieb Daimler.

geometry, and since this showed in his school reports he prevailed upon his parents to let him take his technical examinations.

His first work was in a gunsmith's foundry—this was the time of revolutions and militarism—and he proved to be an expert at his career. But Gottlieb soon found that this manual work was not satisfying his urge to use his alert mind, and accordingly enrolled—as did Karl Benz—for a technical institute.

Daimler did not succumb to the 'steam-engine cult' during his studies. He too was searching for a new method of producing power. Unlike Benz, however, his prime object was to make a unit 'which could be ready for operation instantly' to replace the slow-starting steam engine.

After a visit to France and England Gottlieb Daimler took a post at the mills of an old friend of the family and commenced to design tools and turbine power units. Influenced by the engineering advances he had seen at the London World Fair in 1862 he set about mechanising the factory.

Later he joined the Karlsruhe Engineering Works, where he missed Karl Benz by just two years—and met a man who was to influence his life. His name was Wilhelm Maybach. Daimler had seen a spark of genius in him and had taken him into the firm as a designer.

By this time Daimler had examined the Otto Atmospheric engine—and decided to improve upon it. With Maybach as his chief designer he was soon successful. Later, with Daimler's help, Otto designed the first four-cycle engine: dawn was breaking over the internal combustion era.

In 1882 Daimler elected to start his own business at Cannstatt, taking Willi Maybach with him. Here he designed and made his first engine—one that was specifically planned to propel a vehicle. This unit was the pioneer of the high-speed engine. In his design he aban-

The Cannstatt factory in which Gottlieb Daimler produced his early models.

Daimler's 1886 horseless carriage.

doned the known methods of electric ignition and introduced his 'hot tube' system, one that required a platinum tube inside the cylinder head to be kept red hot at all times. At regular intervals fuel was squirted into the cylinder and ignited by the heat of the tube. It proved to be a more reliable method than most.

A modified version of this engine was put into a bicycle; thus

An 1894 Daimler . . .   . . . with weather protection

A Cannstatt-Daimler of 1899. This car was powered by a 24 h.p. unit.

Daimler can claim to be the first man to produce a motor cycle, although in fact he marketed his cars before developing the motor cycle further.

Then in 1885 he secretly installed an engine in a coach, disguising his intent by ordering the coach with full accoutrements for horse-propulsion, saying that it was a present for his wife and that he wanted it made particularly solidly! His genuine 'horseless coach' worked well in the initial tests, which were made in the private grounds of his factory.

But Daimler, with his ranging mind, was not content to confine his talents to road transport only. He built an engine that would fit a small launch, installed it, and became the first man to own a motor boat. This, too, ran successfully: so successfully that it mystified the town's newspapers, one of which reported that . . . *a boat has been seen circulating on the Necker with about eight persons aboard. It appears to be propelled by some unseen power up and downstream with great speed . . .*

Daimler's next move was to develop a two cylinder 'V' engine, a unit for balloon flight, and a little two seater that he called a 'Steel-wheeler'. Later he began to sell his engines—and his cars—abroad, notably to France.

Gottlieb Daimler died before he could see the greatest result of his lifelong efforts, the Mercedes car. It was being developed at the time of his death in 1900 by his son Paul, but was not actually fabricated until after Daimler's demise.

The first Race, in March 1901, in which the thirty five horse power Mercedes was entered was a spectacular show—for Mercedes. It beat all the other entrants from the grid to the finishing line, attaining speeds hitherto unknown. The day of the 'Merc' had arrived.

Soon the term Mercedes, (named after the daughter of a Daimler

Designed by Daimler's son Paul, this model appeared in 1900.

A Mercedes **Simplex**, 1902 . . .

. . . and for racing.

Elegant Baroque. A Mercedes Coupe, 1903.

Mercedes Simplex, 1902 . . .

. . .and for an even larger **family**; 1903.

distributor of some influence) was adopted as the trade mark for all Daimler cars. And today the record of the Mercedes is second to none —a fact aided by their single-minded pursuit of victories in the sphere of motor sport and the advances that it engenders.

And when, long after the death of Gottlieb Daimler, the great firms of Daimler and Benz merged, the world saw an organisation immensely strong, efficient, and dedicated to the advancement of the automobile . . .

1. Prince Henry of Germany in a 1906 car by Benz.

2

3

4

5. Between the wars. The Targa Florio, 1921 . . .

6. . . . and 1924.

7

2. A 1914 Mercedes takes a bend in the 1914 Grand Prix at Lyon.

3. A 1913 Mercedes at Le Mans.

4. A 1914 Mercedes at speed.

7. At the Nurburgring, 1927.

8. In Ireland, 1930.

8

31

wheels, levers and pedals

Is it a signal box or is it a car? The clusters of heavy brass levers, each looking as though they could operate a giant crane, must have confused even the most expert motorist at times. Rows of plungers on the dash had to be plunged, seven-league pedals to be trodden on, gears to be changed in an operation more suited to a crane driver. No wonder this was called the Heroic age of motoring . . .

These levers almost look as though they should be in a main line signal box.

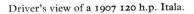
Driver's view of a 1907 120 h.p. Itala.

A tip-up steering wheel on a 1912 Lanchester.

Complexity . . .

. . . and simplicity.

The Veteran driver had much to occupy him
at the wheel of his car . . .

. . . and the Vintage driver's task was no easier! This is
the dash of a 1928 25 h.p. supercharged Bentley.

emancipation

Emancipation Run 1896. Harry Lawson (right) in a Panhard Levassor.

The scene at the White Hart hotel in Reigate as some of the drivers came in for lunch.

Fog, seeping in from the Thames, mingled with exhaust fumes in London's Central Hall. It was November 14, 1896 and pioneer motorists were preparing for the first run to Brighton, the 'Emancipation Run' staged to celebrate the 'legalising' of motor transport and to demonstrate that the motor had come to England to stay.

There were 30-odd cars in the Hall; solid-tyred, tiller-steered, open-to-the-weather cars. Drivers cranked at handles or pulled strings as they battled to start up their engines. Mechanics passed between the cars carrying flares with which to light the burners that heated the platinum tubes that many of the cars used to fire their fuel mixture; few of the cars had starting plugs. Fires broke out in various parts of the Hall where petrol had been spilt but they were soon extinguished.

There was a babble of French and German for many of the cars had been brought over from the Continent.

Gradually the echoes of bangs and back-fires grew, indicating that most cars had been started. They trundled out of the Hall into the drizzle and along to the Metropole Hotel, off Whitehall, where a pre-Run breakfast (tickets 10s, including wine) was being served.

Presiding was Harry Lawson, chief organiser of the Run, the financier who sought to create a monopoly in car manufacture in Britain by buying up every available patent. Lawson and his friends, members of the Motor Car Club of which Lawson was President, wore brass-buttoned uniforms patterned on yachting rig, though one contemporary account said Lawson's outfit looked 'something between the garb of a yachtsman and a Hungarian bandit', and Camille Bollée thought Lawson looked 'like a Swiss Admiral'.

Camille and his brother Léon had brought over three of their racing tri-cars from France—and not without incident. When the cars had arrived at Victoria Station two days earlier the drivers had found they were unable to buy petrol anywhere so they bought bottles of benzine from chemists' shops, tipped them in the fuel tanks and started up.

34

But the smoke and explosions brought a policeman who said the cars could not be driven because the Emancipating Act was not yet in force.

Three horses had to be hired to tow the cars from the station and the drivers had to run a gauntlet of jeers and abuse from cabbies and bus drivers as they went.

Gottlieb Daimler, although a sick man, was also at the breakfast, together with a liberal sprinkling of the aristocracy of the day, and the writer Jerome K. Jerome. A red flag, symbol of the now bygone restrictions, was torn up by the Earl of Winchelsea amid thunderous applause.

At 10.20 Harry Lawson sounded a warning horn. Drivers donned overcoats, capes and goggles. At 10.30 the horn sounded again for the start, and the cars—those of them that could be started—set off along the Embankment and across Westminster Bridge in a trail of bangs and smoke.

It was an adventurous run they were setting out on. There were no garages to assist in cases of breakdown; the motorist could only turn to the village blacksmith for help. There were few signposts then and many of those were inaccurate, and there were no marshals along the route. Crowds were often hostile and likely to throw sticks or stones at the pioneers. And, of course, it was drizzling with rain, which made the roads slippery and the drivers uncomfortable.

Entrants had been given a formidable list of instructions for 'The Motor Car Tour to Brighton'. They said owners and drivers should:

'*Remember* that Motor Cars are on their trial in England and that any rashness or carelessness might injure the industry in this country.

'*See* that their motor cars appear in thoroughly good clean order and are never left unattended on the route.

'*Be* fully provided with sufficient lubricating and motor oil.

'*See* that passengers are provided with proper protection against bad weather, such as mackintoshes, etc., and with light provisions.

'*Use* the greatest care as to speed and driving so as not to endanger ordinary traffic.

'*Treat* the police and other authorities on the route with polite consideration.'

Drivers were told that a stock of oil had been arranged at the White Hart Hotel, Reigate, while water could be had at the Horse and Groom, Streatham; the Wheatsheaf, Thornton Heath; the Greyhound, Croydon; the Windsor Castle, Purley; the Star, Horley; the White Hart, Reigate; the George, Crawley; the Black Swan, Pease Pottage; the Red Lion, Handcross; the Queen's Head, Bolney; the King's Head, Albourne; the Plough, Pyecombe and the Black Lion, at Patcham.

Reigate—22 miles from London—was to be reached at 12.30 and the cars were to re-start for Brighton at 1.30.

At the head of the procession was the Panhard-Levassor pilot car—the car in which Levassor had won the Bordeaux-Paris race the year before. Now it was owned by Lawson, who claimed it to be 'the fastest car in the world'. It carried Lawson, his wife, and a purple and gold Car Club banner.

Harry Lawson, the man who sought to monopolise the British motor industry produced this 'Lawson Motor Wheel' shortly after the Emancipation Run.

A Léon Bollée tri-car of 1895-6.

The cars behind, some of them proudly flying ragged red flags, included another dozen Panhards or Daimlers—one of them being a parcels van belonging to a London store, which was to deliver parcels in Brighton.

There were four Bollées, a fifth having refused to start, four cars made under licence from Benz, an Arnold dog cart, a French steam bicycle, a New Beeston steam bicycle and five electric vehicles including a bathchair!

They kept in station along Lambeth Palace Road, the Albert Embankment, past Kennington Oval to Brixton Road. Then 'Old Number Five', Lawson's 'fastest car in the world', which had been going at walking pace, stopped altogether with overheating trouble. The remaining cars began to race.

In the lead were the Bollées, shooting in and out of the horse-drawn traffic at 30 m.p.h. with their cars rattling like machine guns.

Out into the country they went, the cars sliding on loose stones and muddy roads. Belt drives began to slip. Some cars needed a push on uphill stretches. This was rare excitement.

A reporter wrote in the *Automotor Journal*: 'To rush through the air at the speed of a torpedo boat destroyer, down a narrow, curving road enclosed with hedges and without being able to see what was in front of us, was a novel and thrilling experience. One minute we were 500 ft above sea level and the next only 300 ft. We had accomplished this rapid descent of 200 ft in a few seconds of breathless suspense when the slightest error of steering would have landed us into one bank or the other or plunged us into the midst of cyclists who were waiting at the bottom of the hill to see how we should take the awkward bend.

'We did it magnificently and all the while our engine was actively propelling us onwards and thus adding to the velocity which had been imparted to the vehicle by its momentum.'

At top speed, the Bollées roared through Reigate (decked with a banner saying 'Reigate Welcomes Progress') without stopping for the scheduled lunch. Some others followed them.

At Crawley (where the banners said 'Success to the Motor Car') came the first accident involving a spectator. A little girl who had stepped too far into the road to get a better view was bumped by one of the cars.

More mishaps followed. A Bollée three-wheeler, descending a hill, tried to go between a horse-drawn wagonette and the grass bank. A front wheel mounted the verge, the machine swung round and stopped suddenly, hurling the passenger, W. M. Turrell, into a ditch.

The car carried on, but sand had got into the carburettor and eventually it had to be towed into Brighton behind a horse and cart.

As the Run went on the weather worsened. At Preston Park, north of Brighton, a crowd waited beneath a banner assuring the entrants, 'Centuries will look back upon this, your immortal ride'. Led by the Mayor and councillors, the machines were then driven through a full gale to the Metropole Hotel.

Unfortunately the Run was so loosely organised that no one knows the exact number of cars that took part or the exact number that finished with any certainty. No two reports agree in all respects. The timekeeper travelled in a Panhard which had constant trouble and he was not in Brighton until two or three hours after the first cars.

Electrically-driven vehicles are thought to have entered Brighton first but, as they do not figure on the official list and it is not known how they could have travelled 52 miles on a single charge of batteries, it is believed by some that they were quietly loaded on to a train at Brixton. Similar mystery surrounds two Duryeas which appeared at Brighton, but were not seen on the road down. It is rumoured that at least one car taken by train was muddied artistically on arrival to suggest that it had been driven all the way!

The first two cars to have covered the full distance genuinely appear to have been the Bollées driven by Léon and Camille. Léon's time was three hours, 44 minutes (including nearly an hour spent in reaching Brixton), an average of about 15 m.p.h. Camille arrived a quarter of an hour later. The next car, a Panhard, took over five hours.

A 1901 de Dion Bouton crosses Westminster Bridge in a modern Run.

It was approaching five p.m. when Lawson and his banner showed up, followed by the four-cylinder Panhard of the Paris-Marseilles race driven by M. Mayade, the works manager of Panhard who was later to be the first fatality in a motor race. The Beeston motor tricycle, the Cannstatt-Daimler carrying Gottlieb Daimler, and a twin-cylinder Panhard carrying the Earl of Winchelsea arrived within minutes.

Altogether 14 cars reached Brighton in reasonable time.

The breakdown waggon provided to assist the entrants, a Panhard parcels van driven by Charles Rush, did not reach Brighton until three o'clock on the following morning. Its stock of tools had been employed solely on itself!

When it arrived the great Emancipation Day Run was over.

Similar runs continued until 1902 but not all on the Brighton road, some being to Richmond, one to Oxford and another to Southsea.

In 1927 the run was revived under the sponsorship of a newspaper which gave it the label of 'the Old Crocks' Run'—a nickname which has embarrassed veteran car owners ever since.

In 1928 the *Autocar* took over the promotion under the snappy title, 'International Veteran Vehicle Demonstration Run to Brighton by Cars of the Old Brigade' and this brought it under R.A.C. regulations. After a further year of newspaper sponsorship the R.A.C. took over the run and have organised it ever since except during the war years and in 1947, when petrol was not available.

The ceremony of destroying a red flag was repeated in 1956, Diamond Jubilee Year of the Run, when Mr Wilfrid Andrews, chairman of the R.A.C., tore one up after driving to Brighton in his 1901 Benz.

A competitor drives along Brighton front at the end of a modern Run.

Today a crowd of over two million waits along the route every year to watch the progress of the old cars. Each competitor who arrives punctually in Brighton gets a medal from the R.A.C.—a replica of the one awarded to those who took part in the 1896 Run. It shows the goddess of speed riding in a strangely-designed chariot, clutching a sheaf of lightning and pursued by a racing pigeon. No one quite knows why.

And no one quite knows why the sight of these historic cars so delights everyone who sees them. But they do.

are you an expert?

How well do you know your history of motoring? Try this series of questions; if you can answer more than half of them, you are well on the way to being an expert. The answers are on page 160.

1. How did the name of General Jellinek's daughter become immortalised in 1901?
2. The oldest car in existence to have been restored to running condition was given a half-hour start in the 1954 Brighton Run. Can you name it?
3. What outstanding events of interest to veteran car enthusiasts took place in (a) 1930, (b) 1952?
4. What was the cheapest car ever made and how much did it cost?
5. What was the car registration number issued for the 1903 12 h.p. Panhard of the second Earl Russell that fetched £2,500 in 1959?
6. Who were (a) the Flying Celt, (b) the Flying Mantuan?
7. S. F. Edge inaugurated a racing circuit by driving a Napier at over 60 m.p.h. for 24 hours. Where and when?
8. F. R. Simms took out patents in 1905 for car accessories that are now standard fittings. What were they?
9. For what were these two cars famous: (a) La Jamais Contente, (b) Ford 999?
10. Who were Wilbur Gunn, Marc Birkigt and Henry Leland?
11. Bandits fired on drivers practising for the first new series of races in 1906. Which races?
12. Who was the salesman who became first secretary of a new organisation with a small office in Fleet Street in 1905?
13. The initials FIAT do *not* stand for 'Fires In All Temperatures', as a veteran joke has it. What *do* they mean?
14. Dr Lehwess, a German, tried to drive a 40 h.p. Panhard-Levassor from London around the world in 1902 but in Russia the car froze up, two cylinders cracked, and the attempt was abandoned. Can you name the actual car?
15. What was the speed car that had three Liberty aero engines with a total capacity of 81.18 litres?
16. One car was in production for 19 years—a year longer than the Model T Ford. What was it and what were the years?
17. The first of six cars that were the world's biggest was produced in 1927. It was over 22 ft long with a bonnet of over 7 ft. What was it called?
18. 'Genevieve', in the film of that title, was a 1904 Darracq. But what was 'Genevieve's' rival?
19. Do you know the full name of the first British driver to be knighted for achievements in motor sport?
20. What was the car that Lord Llangattock's son helped to build?
21. Which car was buried in the sands at Pendine after its driver's death?

A 1901 M.M.C. on a London to Brighton run.

A Thornycroft Double Phaeton, 1903.

A 1903 Thornycroft two-seater.

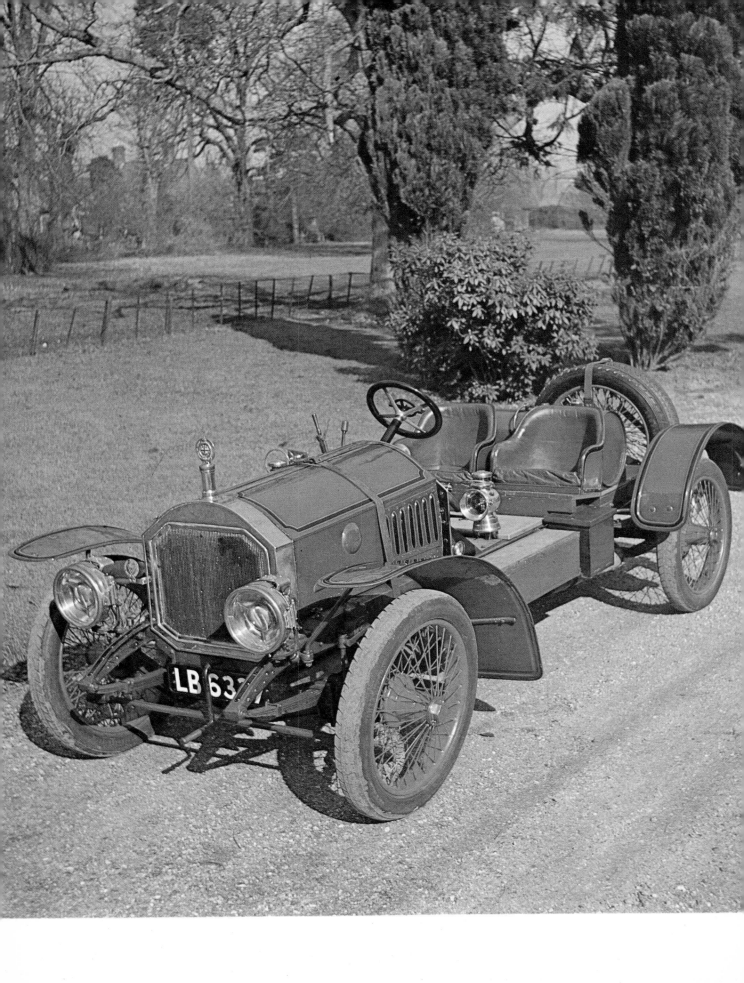

restoration period

Sand racing at Southport, 1930. The Fraser Nash now owned by Kenneth Higgs of Leicester is on the left.

There are two major questions that must be answered: is the car worth restoring, and will it supply the type of motoring the owner wants when it is restored?

A few years ago, Kenneth Higgs of Leicester, a member of the Vintage Sports Car Club, chose a Fraser Nash for his Vintage motoring. His car is a 1930 Anzani-engined Fraser Nash, which after complete restoration has commenced its racing career once again.

In the hands of H. J. Aldington the car had scored numerous successes at Brooklands and on many occasions notched the fastest lap in events. With its present owner it has had an extremely busy time in V.S.C.C. competitions, recently taking part as a member of the Fraser Nash team at Silverstone.

During the four and a half years that it took the present owner to restore the car to its present condition, it was discovered that its chassis, No. 1064, had in fact been part of a two-seater super-sports model issued in 1925, and had been recorded as the fastest non-works car of the time. A pleasant surprise for Higgs: the car was far more historic than he knew.

The records further show that the original car was broken up by the works on 12th February 1930. Then there is a mysterious gap in information. In March 1930, MY 3940 appeared from the works, catalogued as an Interceptor-bodied super-charged Ulster model.

A 1908 Hutton, built by Napiers. It has a 5.9-litre four-cylinder power unit

First time out since the commencement of restoration; rear end . . .

. . . and front end. The exhaust shown was changed as the car was completed.

The choice of a Fraser Nash, said Ken Higgs, is either Yes or No —there are no half measures.

One is either a fan or one detests the very name. Some called it the car with 'four motor cycle engines buttoned together', others say it looks as though it were 'made with a knife and fork'. But Higgs poetically described its vivid acceleration, its delightful gear change and superb handling characteristics, and the unique 'advantage'—as he put it—of sitting over eighteen feet of screaming hot chain.

Higgs was lucky. He spotted his dream car outside a local café. When its owner emerged he saw a pair of feet protruding from the underside of the car—and asked them if they would like to buy it. Three days later a price had been agreed and the car changed hands.

Kenneth Higgs suffered the car's more obvious faults for about a week. It continuously leaped out of gear when on the over-run, the steering box back-lash encouraged the car to move in its own unpredictable direction, and whenever it was parked for more than a moment it deposited a large pool of oil on the road.

The new owner decided to repair some of the faults. The first job he tackled was the oil leak. He removed the sump—and discovered water in the oil. He removed the engine from the chassis in order to check through the block.

And so the job snowballed. At the close of the first weekend's work the front part of the car was in very small pieces indeed.

Abandoning the attempt to restrict his labours to the actual faults in the car, Higgs decided to restore it completely.

His main problem was in fixing the standard of his restorations. One should determine this at the very beginning, he said, for if a single small job is below the standard of the others, the whole operation is pulled down to that level in the final result.

The hardest decision, of course, is to know what to replace and what to leave for further duty—and where to obtain the replacements.

Higgs painstakingly replaced all the necessary parts with accurate replicas of the original components. Searching for these took up a considerable portion of the four and a half years, and, as can be imagined, demanded a saint's patience.

Among the many marathon engineering tasks Kenneth Higgs accomplished, was cutting off the ends of the front axle, building them up again with layers of weld, and boring new eyeholes. New kingpins and bushes were fitted, and the springs re-set.

The engine was also overhauled in intricate detail.

The rear axle and transmission involved some major replacement items for although the chain was easily replaceable, the sprockets were not. Counter sprockets and dog clutches were remade.

Re-covering the fabric body of the car involved the renewal of much of the timber framework, and a tailor's precision when cutting up great rolls of PVC. By the time the re-wiring was completed (the only job that necessitated Higgs calling in expert help), 4,000 man-hours had been put into the car, and nearly half a decade had gone by.

Today the car can be seen in all its immaculate glory, speeding round the circuits of Britain, rejuvenated, refurbished, and a delight to all who behold her.

44

Mock-up of the front end. Higgs said he had to do this occasionally to remind himself of what his car looked like!

Nearing completion. The car has a new dash, bulkhead, and wiring is well on the way.

After four and a half years, the Fraser Nash takes the circuit again. Ken Higgs at speed during a team relay race at Silverstone.

as seen by punch

That British institution, *Punch*, had grown to maturity in the Victorian age, and was some fifty years old when the motor era somewhat shakily began.

Mr Punch had been in a jocular mood for some years. When the bicycle first appeared on the roads of Britain the situations it created were a gift for the humorists. During the 'nineties the pages of the journal overflowed with poems and cartoons, sketches and epigrams about the vicissitudes of the cyclist.

Then in 1896 the motor car took over as the number one Aunt Sally. For ten years the motorist bore the brunt of *Punch*'s humour— good humour for the most part. Technical jokes, allegorical humour, political puns, social jibes, all were put under the satirical microscope of this witty and powerful journal. One of the earliest references to motoring was printed in May 1896. *Punch* recommended that a new safety measure be adopted by the Government. 'A man with a red flag should precede all horsemen!' *Punch*, it seemed was (sometimes) on the side of the newcomers.

No, this isn't a collection of Tubercular Microbes escaping from the Congress; but merely the Montgomery-Smiths in their motor-car, enjoying the beauties of the country. (1901)

THE NEW PROCEDURE
A. J. B-lf-r. 'There! I think we've tinkered it up all right for the rest of this run.'
Sir H. C-mpb-ll-B-nn-rm-n. 'I daresay, Arthur; but you'll have to overhaul it thoroughly before the next trip.' (1901)

HINTS FROM OUR INVENTOR'S NOTE-BOOK
The new 'Motorambulator'. (1897)

46

Soon afterwards it published a poem of a great number of verses, four of which ran . . .

If you desire to travel fast,
A motor car is unsurpassed;
Should you desire to travel far,
Trust not too much a motor car.

And if you're bold enough to start,
Take duplicates of every part:
Two sparking plugs and tumblers twain,
But, chief, a double dose of brain.

'Ware, too, the Peeler; see him stand,
Sneaking at milestones, watch in hand,
To swear your pace exceeded far
The pace that's lawful for a car.

No! Only motorists inspire
Justice with undiluted ire:
For them alone she weighs the scales,
For them alone no plea avails.

BROTHERS IN ADVERSITY
Farmer. 'Pull up, you fool! The mare's bolting.'
Motorist. 'So's the car!'   (1901)

CROWDED OUT
Stage-struck Coster (to his dark-coloured donkey). 'Othello, Othello, *your* occupation'll soon be gone!'   (1903)

47

Some of the names that are part of American automobile history . . . E.M.F.   (1908)

. . . Stearns (1909)

. . . Mercer (1911)

. . . Pierce-Arrow (1917).

american empire

'I will build a car for the great multitudes,' the American pioneer Henry Ford is reported to have said in 1902.

He was a determined man and was as good as his word. He built for the multitudes, and he built greater than he knew, for in 1903 when he created the Ford Company, he could not have dreamt that an empire stretching half across the world would be the result of his labours.

Against the inclinations of most of his stockholders he built a small car—a Model A. It had two cylinders, and developed about eight horse power. Driving power was by bicycle chain, and the engine was under the seat, in uncomfortable company with the petrol tank. The price was a modest $750.

In five years Ford production ran through the alphabet, right up to Model S.

Then came the car that changed the face of America—and world motoring. He called it the Model T.

It was so successful that the demand was soon outstripping production and Henry Ford was forced to instruct his agents to 'accept no orders until further notice' on many occasions. From the time of its introduction in 1908 until it was finally superseded in 1927, the fantastic total of 15,007,033 Model T Fords were manufactured and sold. It was the car that put America on wheels.

The story of Ford is the story of the development of the United States itself. It is the story of a single-minded man, a man who had faith in himself and in his ideas, despite a storm of opposition; an American who built an empire out of the demands of commerce.

Although Henry Ford spread his wings perhaps a little further than his competitors his was by no means the only name in the United States that carved for itself a permanent niche in the history of the country.

First of fifteen million, the 1908 Ford 'T'.

Family outing in a 1910 Ford.

Part of the American scene; a 'T' model in 1915.

Some two thousand different makes of cars have been registered in the Union since 1893, when Charles and Frank Duryea built their first single-cylinder auto. Many of them were small experimental companies; many of them never passed that stage. Names like Elmore, Havers, Jeffrey, Lozier, blossomed and faded in the space of the few years. Curiosities such as the Brownie Karf Dragon, Dodo, are now as dead as—the Mighty Michigan or the Peter Pan.

Some names survive as legends today, tributes to the workmanship and care that went into the making of the cars . . . The White Sewing Machine Company, who built White Steamers, the Pierce-Arrow Motor Company, E.M.F., Stearns-Knight—these names are still seen when the car clubs of America hold their events. Some of these vehicles actually brought about the demise of their own companies—their construction was so solid and skilfully executed, the care in construction was so great, that it slowed down production, and threw costings out disastrously.

But the strong survived. The Reo Motor Car company, for instance—born in 1904 and still fit and healthy—makes trucks at Lansing, Michigan. Studebaker, Willys, Packard, Oldsmobile, Hudson, Buick, Cadillac, were all in existence before the twentieth century was ten years old, and continue to thrive and to grow.

Elegance in the 'twenties; a 1926 Ford coupé . . .

. . . and a 1928 sedan.

Although the motor industry in the United States advanced rapidly in the early part of the century, the conditions of the roads in America did not. A country road in 1902.

Small town, 1924, when in some areas eight out of every ten cars were T models.

Up to the axles in mud, one of the hazards of early motoring.

America was well ahead with flow-line production even as far back as 1914, when this picture was taken.

Assembly methods rapidly improved; this body drop operation was good enough for 1913 . . .

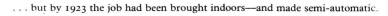

. . . but by 1923 the job had been brought indoors—and made semi-automatic.

The unmetalled surface of most roads at the turn of the century looked something like this.

problems in print

The motoring journals of the turn of the century were wide awake to the new philosophies that the motor car and its revolutionary way of life engendered. The correspondence columns were thrown open for readers to grumble in, and editorials advised, cajoled, prognosticated, and admonished much as they do today.

Some of the items in these glossies of sixty years ago were almost clairvoyant, some of the problems they ventilated are still unsolved. And some of them read like *Alice in Wonderland,* after more than half a century—such as the news flash that told readers 'that the roads are much improved after the recent rains.'

This little prophecy from *The Car* of 1902, for instance, is unusually accurate in parts . . .

'The railway era has done much to change the face of the country and to alter the habits of its people: but the motor car in this era will be a far more powerful agent. It is interesting to reflect what the philosopher of 100 years hence will think of the London of today when he reads of the slow speeds which we tolerate today in our street traffic . . . He will compare with what in his day will probably be entirely india-rubber tyred traffic, propelled by a noiseless

Below left: An essential part of the tool kit in pioneer days. *Below right:* An early Napier advertisement. The industry no longer indulges in name-dropping—or a three year guarantee.

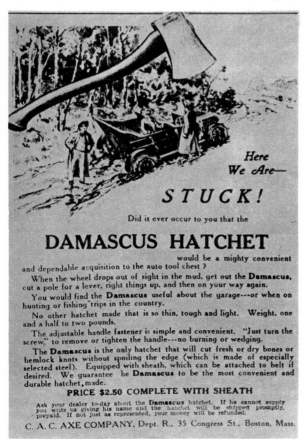

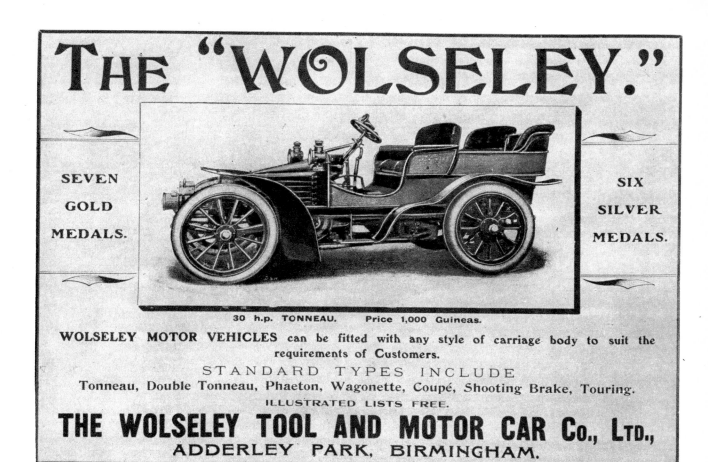

1903 Wolseley, priced like a thoroughbred at a thousand guineas.

mechanism and moving through streets in which there will be nothing but vehicles, for foot passengers will have their own crossings and no longer run the risk they do today of being knocked down and perhaps killed by the lumbering omnibus.'

Then there is this piece of light-hearted advice that is still occasionally the cause of a red-faced motorist being summoned to the magistrates court. It was also printed in *The Car* some sixty years ago . . .

'However fond you may be of the lady, disaster will result if you endeavour to steer with one hand, and embrace your lady-love with the other. Both cars and ladies want your whole attention, and it is better to do one thing at a time . . .'

There were the humourists . . .

'The cost of morot cycling has been stated as a third of a penny per mile. Of course, it depends on the nature of the road. The figure given may apply to an ordinary stretch of highway, but if the scenery of the mile in question happens to be interspersed with policemen the cost is greatly enhanced forthwith.' (*Autocar* 1899) . . . and the humorous reformers. This gem was reprinted in *The Car*, in January 1903. Perhaps it is a blessing that no-one took it to heart . . .

'Will the increase of automobilism go on' (the *Daily Chronicle* asks) 'and occasion a change in tavern nomenclature on the main roads of the country. What can be more incongruous than to see a motor car pull up at some such antiquated inn as 'The Flying Horse' or 'The Waggon and Horses'? The introduction of the steam engine gave the numbers of 'Railway Hotels' scattered over the kingdom . . . but so far nothing has been done in honour of the automobile. Surely it is time the 'The Packhorse Inn' and 'The Jolly Waggoners' and other such reminders of our forefathers, be changed to, let us say, 'The Petrol Hotel', 'The Chauffeurs Lounge', or 'The Motor Palace''.

Then there were the mathematicians, who were also allowed their say in the tolerant *Autocar*. And this leading automotive journal must have been tolerant to let this one in. It is dated October 1898 and refers to previous correspondence . . .

The Pull of the Horse

'Surely, the essential point in the question under discussion lies in the facts (1) that the horse carries his weight himself, and (2) that the weight of the motor is carried by the car. Therefore the motor is able to expend in propelling the car the power the horse wastes in carrying himself, and, consequently, 'horse power' calculated on the present basis is not altogether satisfactory in its application to autocar propulsion.'

The horse-drawn world was not the only faction to hurl barbs in those pioneer days. Motorists hit back with all the force they could muster through the columns of the press. As the *Autocar* of January 1898 bitterly points out, in a quote from a northern newspaper . . .

'A runaway horse attached to a trolley dashed into the side of a tramcar at Newcastle, killing a young girl and injuring four other passengers.' That's all. The noble steed can slaughter and wreck in a couple of lines, whilst a motor car is not permitted to suddenly stop in the traffic under a column and a half *plus* a few bloodcurdling headlines.

In the more highbrow magazines, of which *The Car* was the leader, the academicians had their heads . . .

'Two or three correspondents in *The Times* have been asking why the word *chauffeur* is so often used in connection with the driver of an automobile, when the word from its original meaning and modern application is totally wrong. As I have often pointed out in the pages of *The Car*, 'chauffeur' means stoker, if a real French word is wanted *mécanicien* I suppose would be the proper term to use . . . is it not an insult to the fair sex to suggest that she could possibly be a female stoker for such is the real meaning of the word *chauffeuse*.'

. . . and the legal minds rummaged in The Queen's Statutes. In the item below they rail against a situation that we consider to be part of our present age. This was in 1903:

'*A useful but forgotten statute*. In these days when many of the police are ever on the lookout for offending motorists it should be remembered that it is a statutable offence under the Highway Act of 1835 for a driver of a vehicle that is met or overtaken by another to wilfully neglect to draw to the nearside . . . it may be as well if some motorists took this point up and constantly drew the attention of the local police

54

THE REILLOC PATENT SOLID MOTOR TYRE.

THE TYRE EXHIBITS THE FOLLOWING SPECIAL FEATURES:

1.—All the rubber is above the rim, having free movement in every direction, and being thereby available for its legitimate purpose of cushioning the wheel.

2.—There are no projecting rims to cut the rubber, the side flanges being kept well below the flat iron tyre of the wheel.

3.—The rubber being held by soft flexible fabric which is free to accommodate itself to the movements of the rubber, prevents the wearing action which metal wires cause.

4.—It is a cheap tyre, because of the saving of very expensive material effected by having no waste rubber packed into a rim which is in many cases ONE-THIRD of the rubber employed, and in other cases nearly ONE-HALF, or in other words, there is a saving of from one-third to one-half of rubber.

5.—Another advantage is also gained, viz., greater resiliency, by being able to employ a better and softer rubber than is possible where the tyre is held by the ordinary means.

Please call and see the Tyres in all sizes and sections at the

STANLEY SHOW, Agricultural Hall (King Edward's Hall),
On Ground Floor near Main Entrance.
November 18th to November 26th.

THE REILLOC TYRE Co., Ltd., 122, Victoria St., Westminster, S.W.
Telegrams: "REILLOC, LONDON."   Telephone 625, Westminster.

For the pioneer's comfort. An advertisement for solid tyres in 1904.

to the negligence of drivers of heavy vans who deliberately block all traffic . . . in defiance of both the existing law and the canons of public convenience. These inconsiderate drivers cause a serious obstruction in streets and crowded thoroughfares . . .'

The advertisements of the very early days of motoring were mainly designed to appeal to the intelligentsia, for it was only the wealthy who could hope to purchase an automobile. At first the tenor of even the small insertions was somewhat aloof . . .

'Wanted, Daimler shares—advertiser wishes to purchase from ten to twenty fully paid shares in the Daimler Motor Company Ltd. State lowest price for cash. To the Autocar office.'

'Practical motorists may retain their position in Society by using our Motorists' Hand Cream, which dissolves out black grease from skin-whorls . . . send 1/6.'

CARS FOR EVERYBODY!

"Mercédès," "Automotors," "Panhards," "De Dions," "Cléments," &c., from £50 to £1,100.

MUST BE CLEARED IMMEDIATELY

"Panhard" Car, 40 h.p. (Paris-Berlin) Tonneau Body	£1,100
"Automotor" Car, 10 h.p., latest style, Tonneau Body	£260
"Mercédès" Car, 16-20 h.p., 4 cylinders, 2 bodies (Tonneau and Limousine)	£670
"Orient Express," 6 h.p., splendid condition, solid tyres	£60
"Peugeot" Car, 5 h.p., 2 cylinders, double phaeton, brand new	£100
"Hurtu" Car, 8 h.p., very reliable, solid tyres	£75
"De Dion" Voiturette, 6 h.p., hood and glass, and all improvements	£100
'Darracq" Voiturette, 6½ h.p., dais and glass	£125
"Orient Express," 6 h.p., very fast, solid tyres	£72
"De Dion" Tricycle, free engine	£24
"Hidien" Voiturette, 6 h.p., 3 speeds, 4 places, solid tyres	£45
"Panhard" Car, 18 h.p. Centaure, Tonneau	£800
"Panhard" Car, 10 h.p., 4 cylinders, Tonneau with dais	£330
"Renault" Car, 9 h.p., Aster motor, Tonneau	£150
"Durkopp" Car, 12 h.p., 4 cylinders, new	£220
"Racing Car," 14 h.p. twin cylinder "Automotor" engines, mechanical valves, new	£140
"Gladiator" Racing Car, 20 h.p. (Paris-Vienna), 100 kilos per hour	£235
"Panhard-Clément" Car, 6½ h.p., nearly new, hood	£80
"Leyland" Steam Engine, 6 h.p., on portable frame	£40

The above Cars, &c., are all in splendid condition, and the majority are new. Where not otherwise mentioned Dunlop tyres are fitted.

AUTOMOBILE COMPONENTS, Ltd., 18-24, Church St., Islington, London, N.

New and second-hand car advertisement, 1903.

56

Then the professional stepped in. Advertisements became livelier, more compelling, as was this one printed in the *Autocar* in 1898:

'Don't risk your life in flimsily built cars—
See that you get a strong axle and a substantial frame.
If you don't want to start your motor by turning a dirty flywheel—
If you don't want to have trouble with your coils and accumulators—
If you don't want to require belt dressing—
If you don't want to get any but the best and most reliable coach building—
If you don't want to be stranded because something went wrong with one of your chains—
If you don't want to have the driver's seat on the left—
If you don't want to buy an under-motored vehicle—

ORDER an Orient Express.   175 guineas'

. . . or they appealed to the ladies, realising even then, it seems, that the motoring wife would have the final say in the matter . . .

'Immediate delivery from stock—International Motor Cars, the most reliable, safest, easiest to manage, and handsomest in the world; any lady can drive them; no smell, no vibration, no explosion, no fire; price is from £140: trials at any time: cars on hire. International Motor Company, 15 High Road, Kilburn, LONDON N.W.'

A comment on the suspension of the cars of the early part of this century is unwittingly made by a small advertisement in a motoring journal of 1905. It enjoins the reader to write in for a book on massage. Next to it were two advertisements for well-known motor cars, the names of which are *still* household words.

Just two years after their first car, the Vauxhall Ironworks were advertising widely.

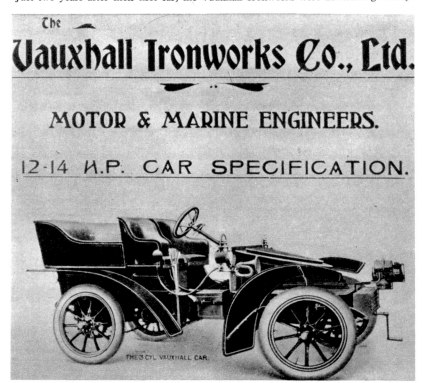

children and cars

They only have to stop for a few seconds and the children swarm around them. Both sexes are attracted to them—the boys want to examine the levers, the strange brass knobs, dials, wheels, pedals, switches, all the thousand and one mysteries of a vehicle that is probably six times as old as themselves.

The girls . . . well, veteran cars, particularly, seem to be female with their light airy build, their spoked and sprung grace, their fringed tops and button upholstery, their fickle ways of steering, starting and stopping when they will. No wonder the girls, too, are intrigued.

And today's children are no different from those of over half a century ago. The intense interest of the young prompted a Victorian motorist to place this placard on his car where all could see it—and refrain from asking the invariable questions:

A young enthusiast in a model that was fifty years old when she was born.

It is an autocar,
Some people call it a motor car,
It is worked by a petroleum motor,
The motor is of four horse power,
It will run sixty miles on one charge of oil.
No, it can't explode, there is no boiler,
It can travel at fourteen miles an hour.
Ten to eleven is its average pace,
It can be started in two minutes,
There are eight ways of stopping it, so it can't run away.
It has to be steered with one hand,
The speed is mainly controlled by the foot,
It can be stopped in ten feet when travelling at full speed.
It carries four gallons of oil and sixteen gallons of water,
The water is to keep the engine cool,
It costs less than three farthings a mile to run.
The car can carry five people,
It can get up any ordinary hill,
It was built by the Daimler Motor Company in Coventry
and costs £370.
We have come from John o'Groat's House,
We are going to Land's End,
We are not record breaking but touring for pleasure.

58

Modern two-wheeler, Veteran four. The older
model is a 1900 Clement Panhard.

Veteran competitors in the London to
Brighton run.

Lord Montagu drives world champion
Graham Hill in a veteran car rally.

Veterans on show at Mr. William Vaux's
garage in Ilchester.

motoring fashion

Edwardian motoring elegance.

For a short while the Horseless Carriage actually pushed the clock back. Coach passengers of the previous era had long been able to enjoy the facility of travelling in their fashionable clothes, secure from the elements in the comfort of a small though luxurious room which was the interior of a private coach.

The introduction of the motor car changed not only the mode but the comfort of travelling. The first automobiles were completely exposed to the elements. Passengers were given the protection of neither a windscreen nor a hood but were expected to be able to put up with the rigours of the weather in the cause of the car.

At first they merely wrapped themselves in anything heavy enough to fend off the rain and wind, or on finer days used riding kit.

But the pioneers soon realised that motoring needed specialised clothing to combat the wind, rain and dust that was encountered at 'the new speeds'.

And since motor cars were nearly all extremely expensive to buy and even more expensive to run, most of these early owners belonged to the former 'carriage trade' class who could afford to lead fashion in their own way.

As a yardstick of the clothing selection of the time nothing can match Harrod's general list. These tomes were produced annually for customers and by 1901 were featuring garments for automobilists, in the saddlery section.

The clothing of the day was designed as a protection against rain, wind and dust, and very functional it was. Most of it was hideous; goggles that comprised two round glass eyepieces in a rubber mount made the motorists—both men and women—look like creatures of another planet ... Scarves or hoods worn around the mouth and neck completed the disguise. Peaked caps, worn by the men, surmounted this mask-like effect, rendering all car drivers alike and giving rise to a great deal of confusion of identity.

In 1909 comes the mention of a 'Foot Sacque Apron'. This was to become the general wear of the lady passenger for some years. An 'apron' of leather or rubber would be wrapped around Madame, completely enclosing her up to the chin. It was, in fact, an adaptation of the coachman's rug. This for the moment filled the gap and coupled with a suitable hood (such as the 'Desirée' which completely enveloped the head, having a mica front to aid vision) the lady passenger could face most British weathers. The driver, however, was forced to wear a more practical leather motoring coat, and though often ankle-length would need the addition of leather breeches, fur-lined goggles and either a motoring hat or peaked cap.

The first windscreens succeeded in keeping only the steering wheel dry, but the intention was there, and soon the coachbuilders were enclosing the passenger's section. The unfortunate chauffeur, however, was still the 'man outside' and it was he who still had the weather to combat. Hence the considerable range of clothing available soon

Matching coat, dress and hat, 1902.

after the turn of the century for him. Chauffeur's breeches, for example, could be had in wide varieties of tweed, whipcord, melton, doeskin and Bedford cord. A note in the Harrod's list adds, 'Brass livery buttons extra.' These were offered to the chauffeur with the owner's personal crest and family motto at 45/- a pair. It was assumed that any client who could afford these would automatically have a family motto as no prices were quoted without them!

About 1910 came the Aerosmoc—the forerunner of the siren suit, and one 'greatly appreciated by the aeroplanist and the driver of racing cars' as it was put at the time.

But the Aerosmoc was short-lived and the reason was that it was practical—and looked it. For by now the majority of motorists were enclosed and no longer needed practical clothes. The Edwardians could resist the temptation no longer; almost overnight, motoring clothing became Fashion.

Mention should be made of the important part that fur played in the motorist's wardrobe. It was hardly necessary to add in advertisements for coats, helmets, caps and even goggles that they were all fur-lined. A fur-lining to the motorist was his assurance of at least some comfort on his draughty expeditions. But not just any fur: the early motorist wanted the best. Even up to 1929 Harrod's listed motoring rugs in Black Goat, Sable Goat, Grey Goat, Red Fox, Grey Fox, Grey Wolf, Jackal, Electric Seal, Kangaroo, Racoon, Marmot, Musquash and three kinds of possum!

Fur was used in all the gloves and gauntlets for the Edwardian driver. Gloves were gauntlet size and gauntlets were big enough to hide in. Though the driver's feet had to be relatively free to operate the pedals, his lady passenger, in 1912, was offered the 'Grey Fox Foot Muff' at 21/-. Lined in Iceland Sheep, the Fox fur cover was guaranteed to include the head and brush—nobody quite knows why.

Perhaps 1912 could be called the year of change, for it was around that time that lady motorists realised that going for journeys by car not only took them from place to place but also ensured that they were seen by those who mattered. Hence the motoring creations that were made at the time—some so ornate that it must have been difficult

DEA EX MACHINÂ. THE GODDESS OUT OF THE CAR.

"But what is this? What thing of sea or land?
Female of sex it seems,
That so bedecked, ornate, and gay,
Comes this way, sailing
Like a stately ship.
         *   *   *
An amber scent of odoriferous perfume
Her harbinger."—MILTON, Samson Agonistes.

to preserve them for the length of a journey. Dresses became more dressy, finery became finer, and hats no longer even pretended to be a form of protection for the lady owner.

In the 'Modes and Motoring' section of an early copy of *The Car*, 'Mondaine' writes breezily:

. . . Messrs. Dunhill of Conduit St., W., may be given credit for some advanced ideas in motoring millinery. The 'bonnets' they are showing at the moment are perfectly delightful—so dainty and charming and wonderfully becoming that I think most of us will invest in a couple of these selfsame models once we have seen them. But let me particularise. Model No. 4130 is, perhaps, the prettiest of all. Here a soft ninon in one shade is closely ruched over silk in a contrasting colour. Velvet forms the crown, and under the brim of the close fitting shape there is a fascinating cap of gathered silk and ninon. Small satin roses are added round the bonnet, which forms a complete protection against wind and dust . . .

One feels that 'Mondaine' was forced to add the last line to give her fashion piece at least some significance in a motoring magazine.

The First World War brought an end to such ostentation and when peace returned it was found that the peak of motoring fashion had passed—motoring clothing was on the way out as the saloon came in.

By 1910 a new branch of the fashion industry catered for the female *motoriste*.

65

bodies beautiful

It was inevitable that the first motor cars resembled their horse-drawn predecessors. Centuries of design had made traditional the basic design of the coach, with its driver's seat in front and a well-shaped passenger compartment slung between the wheels.

When the petrol engine burst upon the scene no one quite knew where to put it. Some installed the ironmongery under the driver's seat, others placed it at the rear of the vehicle; occasionally it could be found at the front end. This gave rise to a complexity of body styles, some of which were elegant, some flamboyant, and some rather curious . . .

Above left: The first motor cars resembled their horse-drawn predecessors. This is a Landau.

Above right: A Vis-à-Vis, by Benz.

A Phaeton, 1898.

A 1900 Benz Dogcart at Hyde Park.

Right: A Curved Dash Runabout by Oldsmobile, 1924.

A Georges Richard Landaulette of 1903 . . .

A cartoonist sees the taxi of the future in 1897 . .

. . . and by 1905 his humour is fact. This amazing vehicle is a hansom cab.

67

Panhard-Levassor's Covered Tonneau, 1902.

A Mercedes two seater. The driver is B.B.C. commentator Peter Dimmock.

A Forecar by Riley, 1903.

A family Wagonette by Wolseley, 1904.

The name is Liliputwagen, and the year, 1905.

Vauxhall Estate Car, 1910.

A Limousine. This is a 1910 50 h.p. Wolseley.

From a catalogue of 1911.

Daimler coupé, 1915.

Curiouser and curiouser. A 1915 Daimler 'special'.

brooklands

At the beginning of the century motor racing was flourishing on the Continent. But here the sport was hobbled, for Britain refused to allow racing on the public roads as Continental countries did.

Then Hugh Locke-King, a rich business-man, built Brooklands and the picture changed radically. Locke-King was a motoring enthusiast of great fervour. He spent a quarter of a million pounds on his project—the first permanent motor racing circuit in the world—without thought of reward other than the encouragement of British motor development.

The site was near Weybridge in Surrey on land he owned. It was a tremendous operation. Thirty acres of woodland had to be cleared. The River Wey had to be spanned. Neighbouring property owners did their best to balk the plan.

But Locke-King was determined. An army of 2,000 men, using 200,000 tons of concrete, completed the circuit in nine months, and it opened early in 1907. It was a concrete ribbon nearly three miles long, roughly pear-shaped, with two straights connected by bends sharply banked for speed. There was a grandstand, and tunnels under the track to allow spectators to cross to the other side of the circuit.

S. F. Edge's Napier (left) and his pacing cars line up at Brooklands before his attack on the 24-hour record.

Even before the official opening Brooklands was involved in motoring history. Selwyn Edge of Napier cars booked the track for an attack on the 24-hour record. It was then held by America with 1,096 miles covered in the time. Edge's aim was not only to improve on that distance but to drive at over 60 m.p.h. for the whole 24 hours. Many scoffed at the idea.

But Edge went ahead with his plans. His car was a green 7¾ litre Sixty Napier and he was to be accompanied by two similar models, one red and one white, to pace him and relieve the boredom of the long drive.

He began at six in the evening. He had selected this time so that he could get the night driving done while fresh. In his first hour he covered 70 miles. Then darkness closed in and the acetylene lamps of the Napier were lit. So were 300 lanterns around the circuit which Edge bought and borrowed from all over England.

70

Artist Gordon Crosby's impression of Edge during his epic drive in June 1907.
(Courtesy *The Autocar*)

By their light he roared on, putting in 72 miles in his best hour and never less than 61 in his worst. Rain soaked him, for the Napier was an open car, and a stone shattered his windscreen but he kept going to complete 1,581 miles at an average of 65.9 m.p.h.

Edge's magnificent feat created wonderful advance publicity for the racing which began the following month. The first races were organised like horse races. Cars were not numbered; the drivers wore coloured smocks like jockeys. Each race was a 'Plate' and prize money was in sovereigns.

The first day was not without incident. The carburettor of a Minerva burst into flames and the bonnet of an Ariel Simplex flew off, leading to a rule making bonnet straps compulsory. People living nearby renewed their opposition, complaining that fumes from the cars ruined their raspberry crops.

Racing went on, of course, but before the first season ended there were fresh ammunition for the critics. Vincent Herman, driving the Minerva that had caught fire, took a turn too fast, the Minerva's front wheels collapsed and the car turned over. The mechanic was thrown clear but Herman was pinned beneath the car and killed.

Next season there was another death when a Mercedes hit the parapet of a bridge and the car hurtled into the river. This time the driver was saved but the mechanic, William Burke, died.

Lord Lonsdale arrives in his Mercedes for the official opening of Brooklands track.

There was more pressure brought to close Brooklands. To combat it Locke-King devised stunts to popularise racing. There were women's races, in which his wife competed, and races for Army officers and journalists, while Edge issued challenges on behalf of his Napiers, the stakes ranging from £1,000 to £10,000.

One successful challenger was Felice Nazarro, who came from Italy with 'Mephistopheles', an 18-litre Fiat, to compete against F. Newton in the biggest Napier, a 90 h.p. Six which had grown to over 20 litres and 212 b.h.p. and acquired the name, Samson.

71

The Byfleet Plate was one of the events in the opening meeting at Brooklands in July 1907. This Napier, driven by Frank Newton, was one of the entrants.

There was some delay in starting because Nazarro had mislaid his black kid driving gloves and declined to race without them or a pair like them. After almost every outfitters in the neighbourhood had been combed, the duel started. The Napier led for the first half of the six-lap race but then a crankshaft broke and the Fiat was on its own.

W. O. Bentley, Malcolm Campbell and L. G. 'Cupid' Hornsted were soon big names at Brooklands. But the circuit was open to all. Anyone could joy-ride round the track on non-race days for the sum of 10s. There was a carefree atmosphere. At night, drivers were known to motor round shooting rabbits from their cars by the light of their acetylene lamps.

But motor manufacturers were also using the circuit for serious research. Sunbeam, Vauxhall, Rolls-Royce, Daimler and Humber took advantage of the high speeds that were possible there—as nowhere else in Britain—to learn lessons about lubrication, cooling, plugs, and tyres.

When the war came in 1914, just after the wearing of jockey's colours by drivers had ended in favour of painting numbers on the cars, Locke-King offered the track to the country and the R.F.C. moved in.

Study in smoke. A grid line-up at Brooklands in Veteran days . . .

The track was never to be the same again. By the time racing re-started in 1920 the years of neglect had allowed bumps, hollows and cracks to mar the surface.

The first post-war race was won by Malcolm Campbell in a 1914 2.6 litre Talbot. (He also won a race against a Matchless motor cycle.)

Then aircraft-engined cars became the vogue. Louis Coatalen pioneered it by building a car round an 18-litre Manitou engine. Kenelm Lee Guinness used it to set a new world speed record at Brooklands, which was now a centre for record-breaking attempts.

The big cars that captured the public's imagination most, however, were probably the Chitty-Bang-Bangs of Count 'Lou' Zborowski They used 23-litre Zeppelin engines on a Mercedes chassis, their crews wore check caps and black shirts and lapped at over 110 m.p.h.

When the Count was practising one day in 1922 a front tyre came off and the car tore down the banking and through a time-keepers' hut. The two men inside ran for a ditch as the car bore down on them; one man reached it safely but the other threw up a hand as he leapt and the car sliced off several fingers.

Eventually cars began to get smaller and more compact; a trend which has continued. Despite Locke-King's death in 1926, Brooklands continued as Britain's home of speed until the second war when the R.A.F. took it over. It was never to return to motor racing.

But the names that Brooklands made, and that made Brooklands, live on in the memories of motor racing enthusiasts . . . Kaye Don, Sammy Davis, millionaire Woolf (Babe) Barnato, actor Jack Dunfee, Earl Howe, George Eyston, Sir Henry Birkin, Whitney Straight, Parry Thomas, the Guinness brothers . . . The name of Brooklands still holds a special magic for all who ever visited the circuit that Locke-King built.

In 1957 Lord Brabazon of Tara, himself a pioneer motorist, unveiled a Brooklands memorial. Built of white stone it stands 14 ft high and its 2 ft high letters, 'Brooklands, 1907-1939', can be clearly read from passing trains: a monument to a heroic age and to courageous pioneers.

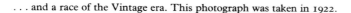

. . . and a race of the Vintage era. This photograph was taken in 1922.

the guards' historic day trip

The War Minister was startled by the plan: the transporting—by motor cars—of a battalion of troops and their weapons more than sixty miles from London to Hastings.

For this was 1909 and the idea of moving an army by motor transport was revolutionary.

The exercise—involving the use of hundreds of private cars—had been thought up by the brash young Automobile Association to demonstrate the potentialities of motor vehicles. Sir Arthur du Cros, M.P. for Hastings and a pioneer motorist, took it to the War Office.

The Minister was impressed and provided the best in the way of troops—more than a thousand men drawn from the Grenadier, Coldstream and Scots Guards. The date chosen was St Patrick's Day, March 17th.

For the A.A. the operation required a major feat of organisation. Cars had to be brought in to pick up the Guards at three points— Wellington Barracks, Chelsea Barracks and the Embankment. (The Embankment detachment was marching from the Tower of London where there was insufficient room for the cars to park.)

The greatest of the many problems was the transporting of the men's machine guns, ammunition, stretchers, entrenching tools and cooking gear. Moving men was one thing, but members could not be expected to risk damage to their vehicles by carrying these unwieldy loads.

Sir Arthur du Cros's brothers, George and William, who operated one of London's biggest taxi firms, came to the rescue. They took thirty cabs off the streets, removed their bodies and replaced them with platforms on which the loads could be lashed.

Two days before the run, snow fell. It looked for a time as though the exercise might become a complete fiasco, with cars sliding into ditches and hedges all along the route. But happily the snow thawed just in time, and the morning of St Patrick's Day dawned fine and sunny. Members' cars trundled to the allotted pick-up points.

A.A. bicycle patrols had been brought in to act as despatch riders between the points so that members' vehicles could be diverted if breakdowns caused a shortage of cars at any point; but, astonishingly, there were no mishaps. A fleet of cars which had been hired to stand by in garages at strategic points throughout London was not required.

All the members who had volunteered to take part in the run arrived as they had promised. The Guards stepped into the cars with their packs and rifles, greatly cheered, no doubt, by this new and effort-free method of travel.

The three columns moved off, to converge at Crystal Palace. Then they headed on to Hastings. Lines of policemen—until now widely regarded as the natural enemies of motorists—waved them through towns and villages and kept back the big crowds of onlookers. For the police had received Government orders to co-operate in securing a smooth journey for the Guards and their transport.

Hastings was reached without incident. There the Mayor and

Fifty years after the first expedition, the Guards travel again to Hastings in Veteran vehicles.

Corporation provided free Irish stew for the Guardsmen while the cock-a-hoop A.A. entertained its member-drivers to lunch at various hotels in the town.

The operation had been a brilliant success. Nowhere were its lessons more closely studied than in Germany, where full reports and maps were published; significantly, German High Command showed great interest.

Many lessons were learnt that day: one of the most amusing was that the caps then issued to the Guards were almost impossible to keep on in moving cars. Many of the men had been forced to adopt a most unmilitary fashion—tying their caps on with handkerchiefs. It was a result of the Guards' run to Hastings that chin straps came into use.

This day trip for the Guards proved momentous in many ways. It had been discovered for the first time that troops could be moved quickly from point to point by motorised transport. Painfully slow horse transport, or three-mile-an-hour foot-slogging had been the only way to move troops since wars began. Military circles opened their eyes to the new possibilities. Motorised warfare was born.

lamps

From the days when lamps were put on a vehicle to be seen by others . . . to the time when lights were designed to see others by. As speeds increased it was necessary to increase the length and power of the beam. From candles to oil, acetylene, electricity.

What have we today to compare with these brass-bound elegances . . .?

Seen at a Northern meeting of Veterans, these imposing lamps range from 1899 to 1915.

A 1904 Cadillac.

Single cylinder Pieper Voiturette, 1900.

A 1903 de Dion Bouton.

A gaily painted 1904 Mors.

the clubs

It could be said that no story of antique vehicles would be complete without including a survey of the Veteran Car Club of Great Britain.

But the significance of this enterprising organisation is greater than that. There would be few, if any, veteran cars in existence at all without the backing and the enthusiasm of the Veteran Car Club officials, and their untiring efforts to restore and preserve these historic motor cars.

More specifically, if it had not been for an informal meeting of three men in 1930, men whose mainspring in life was the motor car, men who were determined to act as its guardians, the public of this country—and of many others—would have been denied the colour and the excitement that these mechanical aristocrats occasionally bring to a life that all too often in this modern age is grey, uniform and uninspiring.

The London-Brighton Run of 1930 was the first to be run under the full auspices of the R.A.C. Previously it has been simply a newspaper stunt, an advertising gimmick. Recognition of the value of the early car, a value greater than that of merely aiding the sales of a journal or newspaper, had been late.

It was not surprising, perhaps, that even the motoring world had not, before 1930, been awake to the importance of the turn-of-the-century vehicles. Many of them were only twenty-five years old: comparable to an immediately pre-war model today. But on November 23rd 1930, the day of the R.A.C. run, three friends, John Wylie, Sammy Davis and Jackie Masters, met for an evening's discussion of the day's event.

Before that evening was over the Veteran Car Club had been formed. Sammy Davis, even then an important figure in motor sport, was appointed Vice President, Captain John Wylie, a born organiser, was made the Honorary Secretary, and Jackie Masters, an experienced motor club man, was 'elected' Treasurer. Between them they put £20 in the kitty.

Before many weeks had passed they had been joined by a number of eminent men, among whom were John Allday, Fred Bennett, S. G. Cummings, and Montague Graham-White, all pioneers of motoring.

The interest of the motoring journals quickened. Advertisements began to appear from would-be owners asking for early vehicles. Through the Press and the embryo club, information and knowledge began to circulate. The cars of the early 'thirties, notorious for their dreary design and poor workmanship, failed to satisfy the genuine enthusiasts and more of the motoring *aficionados* began to buy veterans both as a hobby and as an aesthetic investment.

In addition to the annual Brighton Run other events were organised by the Club. In 1934 permission was obtained to use Hyde Park as a starting point for several events, and a trickle of what one might call the 'lay' public began to take an interest in these sturdy old-timers.

Whilst the coffers of the Veteran Car Club never weighed overmuch (even today the Club is not wealthy) the number of members

Line-up at a Veteran Car Club Rally . . .

grew rapidly during the 'thirties. The original triumvirate of November 1930 had six years later expanded to 187 members, owning between them 100 cars. By the beginning of the last war membership was 250 and vehicles 150.

Today the club has 1,785 members who own 1,500 cars. Time and rust have been defied by this band, and as the years pass more cars are restored to their original sparkling condition. In fact, like a good Cognac, many of the cars actually seem to improve with age, a result of the incredible number of hours expended by owners in cleaning, maintenance and restoration.

By the mid 'thirties it was (due to the high standards set by the Club) a mark of the true motoring enthusiast to be a member, whether he owned a veteran, or merely 'followed' the rallies and meets. The great racing drivers of the beginning of the century were still alive and many of them were eager to join an organisation that had painstakingly built up a reputation of research and technical authority.

. . . and a typical Vintage grid at Silverstone.

In 1939 the Club was flourishing, a small compact band of motoring élite. Then came the war.

Lesser men would have shut down for the duration. But not the Veteran Car Club members. Those whose wartime duties permitted them to spend a little time in club activities used the period to build up a fund for the purchase of cars through the Club, to be sold on a non-profit basis to members at a later date: such was their confidence in the outcome of the war.

The entire administrative records of the Club were bombed out of existence during the war, and in 1945 the secretary took on the marathon task of reconstructing them. Even members' addresses were unknown at the time. But this was one club that had no antagonists; the Press helped, friends and members wrote in with information and donations.

Just after the war the objects and rules of the Club were clarified and cars classified as follows:

(a) Those made before December 31st, 1904, known as Veterans.

(b) Those of not less than thirty years of age, known as Edwardians. (Today this category accepts vehicles up to 1916.)

To obtain and maintain all historical records in respect of such vehicles.

To promote competitions, trials and other events in which such vehicles can participate in their respective classes.

To provide facilities for the exchange of information among members and to act in any way which will promote a continued interest in the preservation of the vehicles, and books, films, lantern slides, records, catalogues and all similar matters concerning them.

Now, in the 'sixties, the vehicles of the Veteran Car Club of Great Britain are part of the British Scene. The Club has developed its traditions, it has a technical language of its own, it has its own pageantry.

And it is the organiser of Britain's largest motoring event of the year.

It gives, above all, pleasure to its members and the public alike. Have you noticed that whenever Veteran cars are seen, they are flanked with smiling crowds? Those smiles are not derisive. They are smiles of sheer delight.

Antique Cars of America

The fifty-two miles from London to Brighton is considered a fair test of Britain's Veteran cars. In America, members of the Antique Automobile Club and the Veteran Motor Car Club have their own Commemoration Run. It is called the Glidden Tour, and is an event run from New York to Detroit—just a thousand miles apart!

Whilst the definition of a Veteran car differs from that of the Veteran Car Club of Great Britain—any vehicle produced before the end of 1929 is classed 'antique'—some of the cars which have successfully taken part in this monumental ride have been of the same venerable ages as those that would be called true Veterans in Britain.

The Glidden Tours, begun in 1905, celebrate no great victory over

Veterans in America. A 1910 Packard 18.

A 1904 Stanley—steaming!

A White of 1916.

stifling traffic laws, no dramatic advance in the speed limit; they had a more materialistic (though no less honourable) reason for their inception.

The first Glidden Tour was organized simply to convey to the American nation that the horseless carriage had arrived as a workable form of transport and was there to stay. It demonstrated—highly successfully—that the day of the railroad as a means of local travel was out, and that the days of the horse were few in number. It took eight Glidden Tours to convince the somewhat sales-resistant public, and finally in 1913 they were dropped.

The three main clubs of the United States are the Horseless Carriage Club, the Antique Automobile Club and the Veteran Motor Car Club. Events and competitions in these clubs are divided into eighteen categories, based on the age and mechanics of a vehicle: today the clubs flourish, sending their members all over the world on sporting events.

Their objects are twofold: to preserve historic and antique cars, and to have a progressive outlook in promoting road safety and opposing adverse legislation.

The Vintage Sports Car Club

No car built after 1930 is worth calling a car—with very few exceptions. Basically, that is the creed of the Vintage Sports Car Club.

And how very right they are! With the end of the First World War the cars that had remained drawing-board dreams for years sprung into three dimensions. They showed that during the war years the industry had been thinking—and thinking hard. The trend was to smaller and cheaper cars. Faster production methods had been evolved during the war, now they would be applied to peacetime purposes. New techniques in making lighter alloys were brought into use, new advances in the theory of the internal combustion engine were tested.

By the end of 1930, these great changes had taken place; in fact

The Vintage Sports Car Club invited two great pre-war Mercedes cars to a meeting at Oulton Park in Cheshire in 1958. This one is the 1937 W123 Grand Prix car.

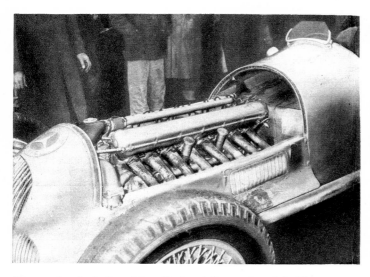

Power units: the in-line eight-cylinder 5½-litre engine of the W125. The output was 646 b.h.p. at 5,800 revs per minute.

The engine of the W163. This twelve-cylinder 'V' unit of 3 litres develops 483 b.h.p. at 7,800 r.p.m.

they had gone too far too quickly. Efficient production methods became mass production methods. Economy of weight became cheese-paring. The cars of the 'thirties, were often hollow mockeries of those of the preceding decade.

The Vintage Sports Car Club was founded in 1934. It was founded on the clear knowledge that the period 1919 to 1930 had brought forth cars that were greatly in advance of those of Edwardian times—production has passed from experiment to refinement—and far more carefully constructed than those of the 'thirties.

The Vintage Sports Car Club allow two other categories of car into their select company; historic racing cars over 15 years old, and certain genuine thoroughbreds of the post-Vintage car.

The work of all these clubs, and of those in France and elsewhere, is of great importance to the motoring world. They have preserved the history and the technical records of the cars of the past. And it is upon the past that the future is built.

. . . and the 1939 W163.

private lives

There are few Veteran cars still undiscovered in Britain. Just occasionally one will surface in some remote barn in Ireland, or an old stable north of the Border.

Bought, used, forgotten, to be recovered, refurbished and cherished once again by an enthusiast . . .

This 1901 de Dion Voiturette is considered one of the smartest Veterans on the road. Originally owned by Sir John Whiteley of Worcester, it was taken off the road in 1913. It was carefully stored for thirty-six years. In 1949 it was taken out again and used in Veteran Car Club events, where it has won a number of prizes. It is in magnificent condition throughout and still bears Sir John Whiteley's crest, the name and address of the makers and the import plate. It has a one-cylinder engine of 4½ h.p.; the brakes are twin expanding shoes, and the gearbox is two-speed.

Still owned by the Vauxhall Company this smart little 1905 three-cylinder car has a rating of 7/9 h.p., is water cooled and cost £200 new. Only twenty of this model were made and this is said to be the only survivor. Some of these cars were fitted with windscreens, but the 'accessory' was not popular in those days—they were described as 'dangerous abominations, unnecessary and in the way during fine weather, and completely useless in the rain!'

A sports two-seater in dark green and dazzling brass, this 1907 Riley has a 9 h.p. two-cylinder 'V' engine, and quadrant gear change. Rediscovered by Major Henry Fairhurst in Watford, Herts, it is thought to be the earliest four-wheeled Riley in existence today.

This pretty 1901 Clement-Panhard voiturette, owned by Major James France, can be seen at all the main Veteran events in the country. Major France found it some years ago under a heap of junk in a friend's stables. He spent a year re-building and repairing the car and entered it in the 1955 London-Brighton Run, when it broke down some thirty times! Its second Commemoration Run had a happier ending; the car developed only one fault—which was repaired with a passenger's hairpin. Its wisdom-teething troubles are now over and today the car is one of the most reliable Veterans on the road.

This 1904 Humber owes its existence to a boy's prank. It had been lying abandoned in a field for twenty-seven years, the plaything of young children, who had stripped it of most of its lighter parts. When Mr J. Gibbs of Exmouth found it he noticed that someone had poured paint down into the engine—preventing the unit from rusting. He rebuilt it to its original specification and has driven it some thousands of miles. It has an 8½ h.p. two cylinder power unit, and is capable of a steady 20 m.p.h.

Once owned and run by a member of the maker's family this 1903 Thornycroft Double Phaeton is thought to be the prototype of the model. It followed the twin cylinder 10 h.p. which was produced early in 1903. The car was bought and restored in 1956 and successfully completed a ten day 1,600 miles rally in Germany the following year. The Thornycroft is a four cylinder 20 h.p. vehicle with multi-plate clutch, 3 speed and reverse gears, and shaft drive. The price when new was £660.

veteran and vintage days

	Motoring Milestones	*World Events*
1885	Karl Benz demonstrates the first successful petrol-engined car and Gottlieb Daimler makes a motor cycle.	Khartoum captured, Gladstone resigns, Lord Salisbury becomes Prime Minister.
1890	Panhard & Levassor begin making Daimler-engined cars in France.	The Forth Bridge opens, Bismarck resigns.
1894	The first motor race—Paris to Rouen—held and de Dion is first home averaging 11.6 m.p.h. in a steam car. The first Benz car is imported to England and Chasseloup-Laubat reaches 39.24 m.p.h. in an electric car.	Japan declares war on China, Dreyfus is convicted of treason, Gladstone resigns again.
1895	Levassor (Panhard) wins Paris - Bordeaux - Paris race at 15 m.p.h. The Michelin brothers fit pneumatic tyres to car. Harry Lawson forms the British Motor Syndicate to buy up patent rights of Daimler, de Dion and Bollée and attempt a car-making monopoly in Britain. Lanchester and Wolseley cars appear.	The Jameson Raid.
1896	The Locomotives on Highways Act legalises motoring in England and speed limit is raised from 4 to 14 m.p.h. Brighton Run is held to celebrate. The first Daimler is produced at Coventry.	Röntgen discovers X-rays.
1897	Automobile Club formed. First Stanley Steam Car produced in U.S.A.	Queen Victoria's Diamond Jubilee.
1898	Riley and Lagonda cars appear.	Gladstone dies. Battle of Omdurman fought.

| 1899 | Jenatzy achieves 65.75 m.p.h. in electric car. The Automobile Club hold Richmond Motor Show at which Humber, Sunbeam and Napier appear. | Boer war begins, Ladysmith besieged. Marconi experiments with wireless telegraphy and Dreyfus is pardoned. |

In 1900 the Automobile Club held its 1,000 Miles Round Britain Trial.

| 1900 | The Automobile Club holds Round Britain Trial. The first international races—for the Gordon Bennett Cup—begin. There are now 209 different makes of cars, half of them American. The first National Automobile Exhibition held in U.S.A. | Mafeking is relieved, Lord Roberts enters Pretoria. Boxer rebellion in China. |

| 1902 | S. F. Edge (Napier) wins the Gordon Bennett race for Britain for the first time. Henry Ford makes his first car for sale. | Edward VII is crowned, the Boer war ends, Education Act passed. |

| 1903 | The Motor Cars Act requires registration of cars and carrying of numbers and raises speed limit to 20 m.p.h. Accidents in Paris-Madrid race end Continental city-to-city races. Ford sells his first car. | The Wright Brothers fly at Kitty Hawk. |

1903: Henry Ford sold his first car, Model 'A'.

| 1904 | Frederick Royce makes first car, Rigolly puts world land speed record over 100 m.p.h. Ladies' Automobile Club formed | Russo-Japanese war begins. Franco-British pact. |

| 1905 | The A.A. formed to fight speed traps, first T. T. races held in Isle of Man, a chain-driven Daimler wins first Shelsley Walsh hill climb. There are now 700 car makers and in America they are starting to sell on hire purchase. | Russian fleet defeated and peace treaty signed. |

91

Rolls-Royce produced the first Silver Ghost in 1906. This is the factory at Cook Street, Manchester, where they were made.

1906	Rolls-Royce produce Silver Ghost.	San Francisco earthquake.
1907	Brooklands opens and the Automobile Club becomes Royal.	Old Bailey opens, New Zealand becomes a Dominion.
1909	Ford sells 10,000 cars in a year.	Blériot flies Channel and Old Age Pensions are introduced. Union of South Africa is constituted.
1910	The British Government introduces tax on horse power and promises the Road Fund will be used to improve roads system.	King Edward dies and is succeeded by George V.
1913	First Morris car makes début.	Britain gets news of disaster to Scott's Antarctic expedition.
1914	Motorists give their cars for ambulances.	Britain goes to war with Germany. Battles of Mons, Marne, Ypres.
1915	Petrol tax is raised to 6d per gallon in Britain.	Germans use gas on Western Front; Dardanelles naval action. *Lusitania* sunk.
1916	U.S. motor car production exceeds 1 million for the first time.	First Battle of the Somme. Battle of Jutland.
1919	Vintage car era begins.	First non-stop Atlantic flight made by Alcock and Brown.
1920	British petrol tax dropped but Road Fund tax raised to £1 per h.p.	League of Nations formed. Prohibition comes to the U.S.
1921	Coil and battery ignition begins to replace magneto ignition.	Sinn Fein troubles in Dublin. An industrial depression begins.
1922	Austin Seven makes its debut. Balloon tyres come into use.	Tutankhamen treasures found. Coalition Government ends.
1923	Segrave wins French G.P. in Sunbeam. First Le Mans held. Four-wheel braking established.	Earthquake in Japan. Marriage of Duke of York (George VI) to Lady Elizabeth Bowes-Lyon.

| 1924 | A Bentley wins Le Mans. Car bodies become lower. | Death of Lenin. British Empire Exhibition held at Wembley. |

1924   A Bentley wins Le Mans. Car bodies become lower.

Death of Lenin. British Empire Exhibition held at Wembley.

1926   Chancellor raids Road Fund for general purposes for the first time. The British G.P. held at Brooklands. Spare wheels are now carried vertically at the rear of cars.

General Strike. Germany becomes a member of the League of Nations.

1927   Segrave makes land speed record 203.79 m.p.h. The Model T Ford is replaced. Roof lines begin to curve.

Lindbergh flies Atlantic alone.

1928   New petrol tax in Britain: 4d per gallon. Synchromesh gears invented.

British women get the vote. Kellogg Pact to outlaw war is signed.

1929   Segrave makes land speed record 231.44 m.p.h. and is knighted. Passenger car production in U.S.A. reaches 4,587,400, a record figure until 1949 when production rose to 5 million.

Vesuvius erupts. Graf Zeppelin sets records. British forces evacuate Rhineland.

1930   New Road Traffic Act abolishes 20 m.p.h. British speed limit and introduces compulsory Third Party Insurance. Daimlers fit cars with fluid flywheel drive and running boards begin to disappear.

R 101 disaster.

1908: Model T Ford

lady driver

Mrs Edward Kennard.

'Mrs Edward Kennard—a pioneer automobilist, a daring rider to hounds and an expert wielder of the rod.'

That is how the lady is described by the *Lady's Pictorial*; Mrs Kennard, for all her starched Edwardian appearance in photographs was something of a dare-devil. In 1905 she was interviewed by the magazine and we learn from her replies not only about the lady herself but also something of the outlook of motorists of that era.

The journalist took his life in his hands and interviewed Mrs Kennard while she drove her Darracq along the Northampton Road. 'There is room in life for more interests than one,' Mrs Kennard began, 'and I like my motors as much as my horses. They present as many problems to solve, like all mechanisms, and to solve problems —to dive into the unknown—is delightful.'

Having dealt with the new entertainment with such enthusiasm, Mrs Kennard turned to the maintenance of her machines. Cleaning and servicing, she claimed, was all done by herself, and she agreed that 'considerable exercise of muscular strength' was necessary to remove the tyres.

'Pumping up is a big business, and I took 200 strokes to fully inflate the tyre on my husband's Napier.'

'And can you do the usual roadside repairs?' asked the correspon-

The Napier on which the intrepid Mrs Kennard experienced her fastest drive.

dent of the *Lady's Pictorial* from the passenger seat in the Darracq.

'On a motor bicycle, yes: such as shortening, removing and putting on belts, grinding valves, attending to the ignition and carburettor.'

It can be seen that this sort of work was considered not only in the class of 'running repairs' but also work that could well be done by the lady driver, a fact which no doubt produced a far more independent breed than today's motorist—male or female.

'She seems speedy for a 15-horse,' said the passenger.

'She averages 30 m.p.h.,' said Mrs Kennard with pride. 'Darracqs are very fast and although only nominally 15 horse she develops much more on the brake. My first car was a 3½-horse Benz, of which I was fearfully proud, as in 1890 not only were cars still something of a curiosity, but in Market Harborough and its environs, it was practically unknown. What an abomination of desolation my little Benz was considered! But what pleasure I got out of it to be sure. Brooks and I used to spend hours mastering the details of its internal economy, and taking long drives, much to the amazement of the country folks, who considered us hopelessly demented.'

'My next car was a 4½-horse Progress car, with a de Dion motor, which is quite the best engine for a small car. Then, wishing for more speed, I got another Progress with a 9-horse de Dion. My husband presently caught the fever and had the first Napier ever running on the road. It was a 9-horse, and was entered for the first reliability trial in 1900 when, driven by Mr S. F. Edge, it won the International Gold Medal.'

Part of the Irish Gordon Bennett course.

These three cars started a spell of motoring enthusiasm which took the adventurous Mrs Kennard through five cars, four motor cycles and one motor tricycle.

'What is the fastest car you have been on?' Mrs Kennard was asked.

'Colonel Mark Mayhew's 100-horse Napier,' she said as she turned her Darracq into the drive of 'The Barn,' her country seat. 'We went over to the Isle of Man to see the Eliminating Trials, and the Colonel took me over the course in his racer. I held a strap in my hand, sat in the mechanician's seat and kept my feet firmly pressed against a specially constructed footboard in order to maintain my balance. The speed was terrific and the pressure of air seemed to force my head right back. Rounding the corners was an experience not to be forgotten'.

'We went over to Hamburg to see the race, but, like most of the people on the grand stand, did not succeed in doing so. The Irish Gordon Bennett was much more interesting, as one did have the opportunity of knowing what the racers were doing.'

From here the interview turned to Mrs Kennard's successes on the hunting field, but she was first asked which she preferred; hunting or 'Automobiling'. Mrs Kennard's answer seems to sum up the idea of the motor car at that time as an amusement rather than a means of transport.

Answered Mrs Kennard, 'Both equally well. Neither interferes with the pursuit of the other. One hunts in cold damp weather and when it is dry and hot, one motors. To each its appropriate time.'

95

genevieve

A great part of today's great interest in veteran cars must be credited to the film *Genevieve*. Before the film was made only a limited number of enthusiasts were interested in the pioneer motors; after *Genevieve* they became a national enthusiasm.

The film, made in 1952, took for its theme the annual London to Brighton run, and the fictional story, by William Rose, related the adventures of a young couple who took their 1904 Darracq, the 'Genevieve' of the title, on a run. They became involved in a wager with the owner of a 1905 Spyker which called for a race back to Westminster Bridge.

John Gregson and Dinah Sheridan were the couple in the Darracq; Kenneth More and Kay Kendall the Spyker crew.

After some preliminary skirmishing over details in the script, the Veteran Car Club co-operated enthusiastically in making the film. At first, Henry Cornelius, the South African born producer, intended to have British cars as the objects of the rivalry—a Lanchester, and a Wolseley or Humber—but for various reasons such cars were either unsuitable or unobtainable at the time.

Finally Norman Reeves, a car distributor and well-known Veteran owner, agreed to lend the Darracq, and another enthusiast, Frank Reece, lent the Spyker.

'Genevieve' was a 12 h.p., two-cylinder two-seater which had cost £350 when new. The Spyker, the only Dutch car in the Veteran Car Club, was a four-cylinder four-seater of 12/18 h.p., which had sold at £460 in 1905.

For nearly three months the two cars were driven over the roads of southern England by the stars of the film while the cameras turned. John Gregson was, in fact, a learner driver, and had not taken his driving test at the time, but happily he had no difficulty in coping with the Darracq's complex three-speed gearbox. The police co-operated by turning a blind eye to the absence of 'L' plates.

The Darracq and the Spyker ran faultlessly throughout their film

The 1904 Darracq 'Genevieve' starts on her momentous Brighton Run.

Rivalry on the Brighton Road. *Left to right:* Dinah Sheridan, John Gregson, Kenneth More, and Kay Kendall.

Women-power aids horse-power.

career, with none of the troubles that they experienced in the fictional film story. In fact they were so reliable that it was suggested—quite seriously—that they should tow the film company's modern generator truck when it refused to start one frosty morning!

Nearly 40 members of the Veteran Car Club also lent their cars for scenes in the film, driving them themselves. For scenes in Hyde Park, starting point of the Brighton runs, thirty-five members drove up in their veterans. Many also took their cars to Brighton for shooting there.

To add authentic atmosphere, the film men also took shots of the actual Brighton Run of 1952 and wove them into the picture.

The final result was brilliant. Cornelius had provided something for all . . . romance between the couples, comedy, with Kay Kendall's trumpet-playing scene an unforgettable high spot, excitement in the no-fouls-barred race. And he had also managed to satisfy the serious-minded motor enthusiast.

The film, which made Kenneth More a star actor, was acclaimed everywhere. People who could not tell a baby Austin from a Stanley Steamer flocked to see it. The film went the rounds and was reissued

The Spyker arrives at Brighton.

The Darracq enters London on its rim . . .

. . . closely pursued by the Spyker.

—again and again. Manufacturers rushed out ash trays, beer mugs, cuff links, calendars, greetings cards—all bearing reproductions of veteran cars.

The film was sent abroad, where it met with the same success. All over the world it awakened interest in old cars. America staged 'Genevieve Rallies'—even a 'Brighton Run'—from Denver to Brighton, in Colorado. In Australia, in Holland, France and Germany there were runs based on the London to Brighton event.

'Genevieve' is no longer with us to take part in the Brighton run. Norman Reeves sold the country's most famous motor car—for a figure in the region of four times its cost when new—to a New Zealander, and caused an upset among members of the Veteran Car Club bitterly opposed to allowing any historic cars to leave the country.

But Reeves was tired of being called 'Mr Genevieve' and of hearing jokes about his car—a film star vehicle that had become top box-office all over the world.

Peter Sellers and Cyril Cusack in the film *The Waltz of the Toreadors*) The car is a 1904 Tony Huber.

Cadillac, 1906.

An early 20th-century taxi.

Model T Fords at a rally.

British traditional: the Classic Riley front end.

the record breakers

What is the great lure of speed? What compels men to drive into the mouth of danger year after year, to shave a few split seconds off a speed record? Sir Edmund Hillary gave a classic answer when he was asked why he had to climb Everest. 'Because it is there!' he said.

And so it is in the field of motoring. Since the first clumsy engine was fitted into a coach, the urge to travel faster than ever before has been there. The determination to raise the speed record another notch will never flag while the challenge exists.

A Frenchman, the Comte de Chasseloup-Laubat, began it. Driving a Jeantaud electric car on a stretch of road at Achères, near Paris, in 1898, he put up the first generally recognised world land speed record. The speed: 39.24 m.p.h.!

After this the struggle to be the fastest man on wheels was on. In the months that followed the Comte duelled with Camille Jenatzy, a young Belgian nicknamed 'the Red Devil' because of his red beard and hair, a racing driver who thrilled crowds with his driving but seldom finished a race.

Jenatzy had his own tiller-steered electric car, 'La Jamais Contente', which he had streamlined into cigar shape. He reached 41.42 m.p.h. The Comte replied with 43.69. Jenatzy pushed the record up to 49.92. The Comte made it 57.60.

Then, in 1899, Jenatzy became the first man to beat the mile-a-minute barrier. In motoring's earliest days some experts had forecast that the human frame would not stand up to a speed of over 60 m.p.h. But Jenatzy reached 65.79 m.p.h.—and remained healthy.

After this electric cars with their limited power were out as far as the record was concerned. In 1902 Léon Serpollet puffed along Nice's Promenade des Anglais in a steam car of his own design to push up the record to 75.06 m.p.h. American millionaire W. K. Vanderbilt beat this with 76.08 m.p.h. in a petrol-engined Mors at Ablis, near Chartres, and before the year was out a similar Mors had achieved 77.13 m.p.h.

The next year a Gobronne-Brillie with a four-foot-long, four-cylinder, 15-litre, 100 h.p. engine, was clocked at 84.73, and in 1904 Henry Ford, the American manufacturer, passed the 90 m.p.h. mark for the first time in the United States with his Ford 999, a four-cylinder car with no gears and no clutch. He was unfortunate: his speed was timed by an American club at 91.37 m.p.h. but due to a hitch in the arrangements this figure was not recognised by European authorities.

A fortnight later, obviously spurred by Ford's success, W. K. Vanderbilt took a 90 Mercedes over Daytona Beach, Florida, at 92.30 m.p.h. but this was also denied world recognition. Then the Gobronne-Brillie, driven at Nice by Rigolly, achieved 94.78 m.p.h., and two months later Baron Pierre de Caters drove his Gordon Bennett Mercedes along Ostend promenade at 97.26 m.p.h. The 'ton' was approaching. The so-called experts had been confounded: the human body, it seemed, could stand up to considerably more buffeting than was expected.

Jenatzy beats the mile-a-minute barrier in his 'Jamais Contente', in 1899. From a painting by Gordon Crosby. (Courtesy *The Autocar*).

The magic figure was to fall to Rigolly and the Gobronne-Brillie at Ostend. The car with the chisel-shaped bow reached 103.56 m.p.h. But even that respectable figure was not allowed to stand for long. Before 1904 was out, Barras in a Darracq 100 h.p. car achieved 104.52, also at Ostend.

Britain, due to the slow start of its motor industry, had not taken part in the record breaking up to this point, but in 1905 Sunbeam sent S. F. Edge's six-cylinder 90 m.p.h. Napier to Daytona Beach's Speed Week. Despite the bumpy nature of the sand the driver, Arthur Macdonald, hit 104.65 m.p.h. but, although this was accepted in America, the figure was again denied European recognition.

In 1906 Frank Marriott drove a Stanley steamer at 121.57 m.p.h. at Daytona to create the last steam-held record.

Three years passed and Victor Hemery, who had reached 109.65 on the Arles road in 1905 with a V8-engined 200 h.p. Darracq, established the first record on British soil. He drove a big four-cylinder Blitzen Benz at Brooklands, opened two years earlier, at 125.95 m.p.h.

Until this time one-way speeds had been accepted, but now, to counter tail-wind and downhill gradient assistance, it was agreed that record speeds should be then taken on the average speed of two runs in opposite directions; consequently speeds fell slightly.

Just before the First World War, L. G. 'Cupid' Hornsted brought the record back to Britain with a two-way run at Brooklands in a four-cylinder 21½-litre Benz at 124.1 m.p.h.

After the war—in 1922—Kenelm Lee Guinness took a giant Sunbeam, powered by a V12, 13,822 c.c. aircraft engine developing 355 h.p. along Brooklands Railway Straight at 133.75 m.p.h. This was the last world record to be set at Brooklands. The straight was too short for faster speeds.

Now Captain Malcolm Campbell came into the picture. He used the Guinness Sunbeam fitted with a new body and longer tail which he called 'Bluebird', the name he was to give to all his record-breaking cars. He recorded an unofficial (hand-timed) 138 m.p.h. on one run.

Next year he tried the sands of Fanöe Island, Denmark. This time he averaged 137.72 m.p.h. but his timing apparatus had not been approved and again his speed was unrecognised. He went back to Saltburn, Yorkshire, after fitting a new body on the Sunbeam but this time the official timing apparatus failed and, though he was hand-timed at 145 m.p.h., the record still eluded him.

Then the frustrated Campbell heard that at Arpajon, France, René Thomas, a Frenchman, had achieved 143.31 m.p.h. in a 10½-litre V 12 Delage and that Ernest Eldridge had done 145.90 m.p.h. in a Fiat.

Back went Campbell to Fanöe Island. At 140 m.p.h. both tyres left his rear wheels. He skidded but kept control of the car. New tyres were fitted. On the next run an offside front tyre came off, shot into the crowd and killed a boy.

Shortly afterwards, Campbell went to Pendine Sands, in Carmarthenshire, hit 146.16 m.p.h., and the record was his at last. The following year he returned to Pendine and increased the record to 150.87 m.p.h. But Campbell now had two formidable rivals. Major (later Sir) Henry Segrave, and Parry Thomas were scouring Britain's seaside resorts for suitable venues for speed attempts.

Segrave went to Southport sands in 1926 with a Sunbeam designed by Louis Coatalen. It was an ultra-modern looking Grand Prix type of racing car with a supercharged V 12 engine of only 4,000 c.c. Despite supercharger trouble Segrave pushed the record up to 152.33 m.p.h.

Then Parry Thomas, 'the Flying Celt', went to Pendine. He used a car of his own make, a giant vehicle with a 12-cylinder 27-litre, 400 h.p. Liberty aero engine on the chassis of the Higham Special once owned by Brooklands racer Count Zborowski. He called this unladylike machine 'Babs' and averaged 171.02 m.p.h. After the runs, to his horror, it was found that a bolt had slackened and the front shock absorber had been loose!

Campbell and Segrave hastened to reply in this dangerous game of leap-frog. Campbell had a dozen or more men working on a new Bluebird at his Surrey home. The car employed a 23.9-litre, 12-cylinder Napier Lion aircraft engine and was the first really specialised world record car as opposed to converted racers. For Segrave, Sunbeam were building a new car in which he would sit between two 500 h.p. Matabele aircraft engines.

Campbell was ready first. In January 1927 he went to Pendine. Again he suffered reverses. On the first day the car crossed some soft sand and began to sink. A lorry and 60 helpers prised it free just before the tide came in. Next day he did 135 m.p.h. Two weeks later he returned and was travelling at over 170 m.p.h. when a shell slashed a rear tyre and caused him to skid. The beach was hand-cleared of all sharp stones and shells. Then he made a run at 180 m.p.h. On the return run a bump shot him in the air, the wind whipped away his goggles and sand blasted his face, but he managed to complete the course and set a new record at an average of 174.88 m.p.h.

Camille Jenatzy.

Segrave had decided to take his car to America's Daytona Beach. While it was being crated Parry Thomas returned to Pendine, to attempt a further record.

The late David McDonald who fitted Thomas's tyres recalled in his book, *Fifty Years with the Speed Kings* that Thomas had been suffering from influenza. He was impatient and on edge, but insisted on making a run. When he was travelling at nearly 170 m.p.h. the offside driving chain broke, smashed through the windscreen and decapitated him. The car turned over and burst into flames. It was later buried ceremonially in the sands where Thomas died in the quest for speed.

Segrave heard the news on board ship on his way to Daytona. Immediately, he had his chains thoroughly overhauled, but on his first run it was his brakes that failed—he had to drive into the sea in order to slow down. However, he made the return run and became the first man to beat the 'double ton', with a speed of 203.79 m.p.h.; faster than the top speed of many aircraft of the time.

Campbell was now working on a new 'Bluebird' using a more powerful 12-cylinder Napier aircraft engine, a 'hush-hush' power unit that had been employed in the Schneider Cup-winning Gloster aircraft. The car also had a large vertical tail fin to act as a stabiliser.

In February 1928 he followed Segrave's route to Daytona, and, after his usual ill luck, set a new record of 206.96 m.p.h.

The Americans had become a little nettled at British supremacy in record breaking, particularly as many of the records were created in their own country. Two American contenders were now ready. They were Frank Lockhart, with 'Black Hawk', a Stutz with a three-litre, 16-cylinder engine and a cigar-shaped shell, and Ray Keech, with the 'Triplex', a four-ton brute built by J. H. White, a Philadelphia sportsman. It had three Liberty aero engines, one in front of the driver and two side by side behind him. They gave a total capacity of 81 litres!

Parry Thomas in 'Babs'.

Sir Henry Segrave's 1,000 h.p. Sunbeam. This car took the World Speed Record to 203.79 m.p.h. in 1927.

A few days after Campbell's achievement Keech had clocked 207.5 m.p.h., and Lockhart had been killed by his car.

At the end of 1928 both Campbell and Segrave were ready to wrest back the World Record for Britain. Segrave's new 'Golden Arrow' was an Irving-Napier Special designed by Captain Jack Irving, and containing a Napier Lion engine like Campbell's. The enormous car had rifle-type sights along its bonnet—so that Segrave could aim the car on a distant landmark.

Again he went to Daytona and, despite wet sand, averaged 231.44 m.p.h.—nearly 24 m.p.h. faster than Keech. On his return he was knighted by King George V, the first man to be so honoured in this branch of sport.

Meanwhile Campbell was trying a new venue—Verneuk Pan, a dried-up lake in South Africa. It was a costly expedition; the country had to be cleared of bush by native labour and even then Campbell could reach only 219 m.p.h., due largely to rarefied air at the Pan's 2,500 ft above sea level. And so ended the Vintage days, with Segrave holding the record, a record that had been nearly quadrupled in 30 years.

The record was to stay in British hands—those of Campbell and George Eyston and then John Cobb, whose speed of 394.20 m.p.h., established in 1947, remained unbroken until Donald Campbell, Malcolm's son, reached 403.1 m.p.h. in 1964.

fascinating rhythm

Put-put-put, they chug down the highway and turn in to their open-air rendezvous. And the sound of the slow rhythm of a Veteran engine is the music of the Pied Piper to young and old, expert or layman. In they flock swarming around the cars, fascinated, as we all are, by the multiplicity of mysteries that are Veteran cars . . .

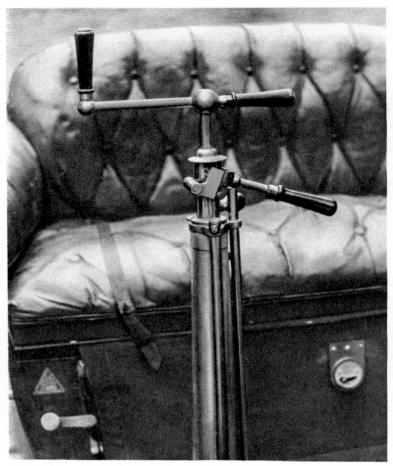

A Rolls-Royce road wheel, 1907.

Steering and gearing in the Victorian age.

One that has been everywhere.

This steamer's cab is more like a bridge.

Around half a century old, but this unit looks remarkably modern.

The Silver Lady.

Pioneer spirit.

motoring organisations

The scene outside the R.A.C.'s first home in Whitehall Court on the day the club was founded in December 1897. Crowds watch a demonstration of the Horseless Carriage.

Frederick R. Simms, founder of the R.A.C.

On a cold December day in 1897 a hundred and twenty pioneer motorists crowded into a room off Whitehall, and the Automobile Club of Great Britain and Ireland, later to be known as the Royal Automobile Club, came into being.

First function of the Club, which was modelled on the Automobile Club de France founded two years earlier, was to provide lists of places where petrol could be bought and batteries charged. It also organised Club tours, members being expected to maintain a high standard of behaviour which included changing into evening dress for Club dinners while on tour.

The Secretary, Claude Johnson, was deputed to arrange races, trials, and exhibitions to demonstrate the advantages of the horseless carriage. And so, in 1899, Britain held its first major Motor Show, forerunner of today's Earls Court Exhibitions.

It was a week-long gymkhana at Old Deer Park, Richmond, where there was a three-laps-to-the-mile cinder track and a grand-stand for 600. The aristocracy, main purchasers of motor cars in those far-off days, turned up in force.

As a curtain-raising stunt that would be widely talked about, the Club had arranged a race between a car and a horse—Gold Ring, which was to pull a racing sulky. The aim, of course, was to show just how superior was the car to the horse.

Unfortunately, as soon as Gold Ring was brought near a car with its engine running, the astonished horse bolted. While it was being chased the Club had to continue with a mile race between S. F. Edge and Charles Jarrott on de Dion tricycles, followed by a slalom run—in and out between posts—and a reversing contest. Then there were demonstrations of trick driving, such as picking up handkerchiefs from the ground while driving.

This involved getting out on the step of the car; one driver fell off but managed to catch and remount his runaway vehicle before it had done any more damage than up-rooting a post. In other events there were several crashes, diversions which did the cause of the motorist no good at all.

Then the Club decided to try the race with Gold Ring again. This time the horse showed no fear and ran well—far too well. Gold Ring

beat a Barrière motor tricycle by half a lap—and the organisers were
horrified. To retrieve the situation they called in S. F. Edge and his
de Dion. Edge won easily enough but it was obvious to the crowd that
Gold Ring's driver had misunderstood instructions about the length
of the race and had pulled up the horse too soon. It was a hollow victory; the Club had to face a third match.

It was a mile race: Gold Ring took the lead at the start, but gradually Edge overhauled the animal. On the third and last lap he drew
level. Then the horse pulled away again and the Clubmen's faces
showed strain, but somehow Edge coaxed a little more from the de
Dion, and the horse and car crossed the finishing line together. The
event had brought no glory to motoring but at least complete
humiliation had been averted.

The expense of the show put the Club's bank balance well into the
red, and a financial crisis was avoided only by the somewhat drastic
expedient of enrolling life members at £25 each—a considerable sum
at the turn of the century.

But the organisation of motor events continued. The following
year the Club staged a 1,000-mile trial starting from London, travelling up to Scotland and back. This ambitious event created national
interest, both in the daily press and, of course, in the motoring journals. Preparation was wide and detailed. Meticulous maps were
printed giving the stopping places for meals (the first was 'breakfast
at Mr Alfred Harmsworth's Country Residence') names of hotels,
petrol points, hills and so on. Distances were given to an accuracy of
a quarter of a mile.

The trial itself did much to prove the motor car as an economical
—if not reliable—method of transport in Britain.

During the R.A.C. 1,000 Miles Trial, the cars were on exhibition every evening
at the overnight stop. This photograph was taken at Bingley Hall, Birmingham.

In 1902, when the Automobile Club moved to offices in Piccadilly, they organised Britain's first major international race—the Gordon Bennett event, held in Southern Ireland. In 1904 they gave a new boost to touring by issuing a hotel handbook listing appointed hotels whose proprietors had promised:

1. That cars could stand outside their hotels free while the drivers were having meals,
2. That hose pipes would be provided,
3. That petrol would be stocked or fetched on request.

The Club organised the first T.T. race in the Isle of Man, and when Brooklands was opened in 1907 they formulated rules for circuit racing on which all rules, throughout the world, have since been based.

Edward VII, the first royal motorist, recognised the Club's work by making it the *Royal* Automobile Club.

But all was not well on the roads as motoring spread. The 1903 Motor Car Act had limited speeds to 20 m.p.h. Police crouched behind hedges with stop-watches enforcing it to the letter. The idea of trapping was offensive to most Englishmen, but motorists could hardly object providing it was done fairly and accurately. However, the pioneers complained that the police methods were often exceedingly inaccurate. Worse, prosecution was becoming persecution, through the nature of fines imposed on convicted motorists. Horse-riding magistrates seemed to be vying with each other to levy the greatest amount in fines each year.

Jarrott's and Lett's scouts setting out on patrol on the Brighton Road.

The motorists' attitude to the police was aptly summed up by these verses, published (anonymously) in *The Motor* in the year 1904:

The village motor trap

Screened by the wayside chestnut tree
The village P.C. stands,
The 'cop' a crafty man is he
With a stop-watch in his hands
And the muscles of his lower jaw
Are set like iron bands.

He goes each morning to his lair
And hides among the trees,
He hears the sound of motors there
And it sets his mind at ease
For it seems to tell of captives—and
Promotion follows these!

Hiding and clocking, summoning,
Onward through life he goes
Each night he's had his vengeance on
Some of his scorching foes,
Somebody summoned, somebody 'done',
Has earned a night's repose.

1905: The first A.A. patrol.

Inevitably the motorists rebelled. Racing driver Charles Jarrott and a friend, William Letts, began operating a trial system of patrols on the Brighton road to warn motorists of the presence of speed traps. Gradually they gathered round them a small band of sympathisers, and in 1905 they announced their constitution under the name of the Automobile Association.

A young salesman named Stenson Cooke (who knew nothing about cars at the time) was appointed secretary at £150 a year and set up in a single room in Fleet Street with a borrowed typewriter.

He enlisted youths on bicycles, lads who normally delivered newspapers to the sellers' pitches, and put them on the Brighton and Portsmouth roads to defeat the police traps: the A.A. defended its members in court free of charge.

The A.A. was a cheeky and defiant organisation compared to the respectable R.A.C. Soon the police hit back. A member of the A.A. was accused of speeding. He said he had not been doing more than 15 or 16 m.p.h. and this was supported by one of the A.A. scouts who said he had followed the car on his bicycle through the trap. But in court the police evidence was accepted. The driver was fined. The Scout was arrested, thrown in Brixton jail and charged with perjury.

To salvage their reputation and to vindicate the society, the A.A. appealed—and won. But the cost was high; members of the committee had to dip their hands in their pockets to pay the legal fees.

THE ROAD AGENCY SCHEME.

The Agent will display a small black flagstaff carrying a movable ball, painted yellow, with the letters **AA** in black.
On the lines of our Cyclist Patrols' Badge, this flagstaff when displayed thus—

will mean

" I AM HERE IF YOU WANT ME."

When displayed thus—

it means
" STOP, PLEASE! I HAVE SOMETHING TO REPORT."

In which case the Member's Badge or Card **must** be shown to the Agent.

Early warning system at A.A. garages in 1906.

However, they continued to strengthen the patrol system. Scouts were armed with badges in the form of discs. On one side of the disc an A.A. badge was shown against a white background; on the other against a red background. When the white side was presented to a motorist it meant 'all clear'; the red side officially signified 'Danger ahead—reduce speed', but quite clearly also meant 'Beware, police active'.

But some motorists, while ready to accept the warnings, were disinclined to pay two guineas to join the Association. So metal badges were made and issued to members to mount on their cars; in future warnings would be given only to members. The warning system was extended by appointing garages and giving them flagpoles. They operated like storm warning cones; if a yellow ball was drawn to the top of the pole it was a signal to members to stop for 'a message'. The message, of course, was the location of the speed trap. In return for this service, members were asked to patronise these appointed garages.

The police naturally brought many cases against the scouts. One

The first A.A. telephone box was set up in 1912.

Shortly after World War I both the A.A. and the R.A.C. mechanised their patrols.
This is one of the earliest A.A. motor cycle service patrols.

was convicted of obstructing the police by showing the red sign of
his badge to a motorist and yelling 'Police'! But on appeal the scout
was acquitted.

He had been operating outside the police trap. The legal ruling
made it clear that the scout was merely warning the motorists to
observe the law, and that there was no offence in his actions.

The police made a new and ingenious plan. One day in 1909
a patrol took up his position outside a trap near Guildford. While
he stood there the police shifted their trap so that when he warned
a motorist he was *inside* the trap. According to the police evidence
he had tried to save a motorist who was breaking the law. The A.A.
could not win this case, but they were far from beaten; they had
foreseen such a situation and were prepared for it.

The very next day they sent out a notice to all their members.
It read: 'When a patrol does not salute—STOP and ask the reason.'
The motorist would then receive a private warning about the presence
of speed traps. Cases were brought against the A.A. but most of them
were unsuccessful. Their scouts were not actually *doing* anything;
they had just been standing to attention instead of saluting!

By the end of the first decade of the twentieth century the A.A.
patrols had developed from a bunch of bicycle-riding youths to a band
of well trained and equipped, khaki-uniformed cyclists soon to be
equipped with motor cycle combinations. The R.A.C. started a
similar service of 'guides' near big towns—the forerunners of their
familiar blue-uniformed motor cycle patrols on the roads. Telephone boxes and free breakdown schemes and other services were
introduced by both organisations.

The growing duties accepted by the patrols—controlling traffic,
tracing stolen cars, giving first aid—brought them into close contact
with the police. Slowly mutual respect and co-operation grew where
once there had been hostility. Motoring—and motoring organisations—had become country-wide and respectable.

new york to paris 1908

The Motobloc, one of the three French cars to compete in the New York to Paris race of 1908.

A brass band played martial airs, and some three hundred policemen struggled to contain a milling, 50,000-strong crowd in New York's great Times Square.

The year was 1908; the date, February 12th, President Lincoln's birthday. But the cause of the excitement had little to do with Lincoln. The immense crowd had gathered to see six cars lined up in the Square for the start of a 13,000 mile, three-continent race for a 'World's Cup' offered jointly by an American and a French newspaper. This fantastic race was to be run from New York to Paris—via Siberia!

The competing cars on the 'starting grid' at New York were an American Thomas, a German Protos, an Italian Zust, and three French cars, a Motobloc, a de Dion, and a Sizaire-Naudin. Each car was fitted out with long range fuel tanks. Each carried a vast stock of tools and spare parts. And each carried a complement of special equipment for this marathon event.

The de Dion, for instance, had steel-studded wheels for use on ice, skis to replace the front wheels on snow, and flanged wheels for running on railway lines where there were no roads. It also carried a mast and sail to convert it into a land yacht!

Ideas on food supplies varied. The Zust crew carried only a spartan stock of dried meat, dried eggs and dried vegetables. The Motobloc crew, in true Gallic style, stocked a larder of fine food and even champagne for celebrations.

The band stopped. A bugle sounded the 'start engines' call. The cars were started, a pistol banged, and they chugged westwards between the skyscrapers in frosty but fine weather.

The American car, lightest and fastest of the six, took the lead, with the Zust and the de Dion behind it . . .

After twenty miles the cars were in deep snow. Shovels were needed to dig them out. It was so cold the crews broke their sandwiches with hammers and thawed out the pieces on their radiators.

The Zust was soon undergoing a string of misfortunes. The radiator cracked. A transmission chain broke. The driver was fined three dollars for frightening a horse. At Rochester a chain wheel broke and every Italian immigrant in the town worked to help the Zust crew.

But 400 miles and eight days out from New York it broke again. Again it was mended. Twice the crew fell asleep and drove into snow-drifts. On one occasion the mechanic even fell asleep in the snow while mending a burst tyre.

The de Dion passed the Zust but, twelve days out, it broke down with gear trouble and the Zust went back into second place.

The Thomas was now 36 hours ahead of the Italian car, the Protos and Motobloc three days behind. The Sizaire-Naudin had given up the race with a smashed differential.

The Thomas passed through Chicago after a fortnight and reached Cheyenne. Here it took to the railway line, a smoother road, but with attendant disadvantages—it had to be manhandled off the line every time a train came along.

Crossing the Rockies the Motobloc fell out; the crew had run out of money!

From acute cold the cars passed into the extreme heat of the Nevada desert. Patriotically, the Thomas was still leading the Zust, de Dion and Protos.

In Death Valley the de Dion bogged down in loose sand. The driver set out to seek help, met an aged prospector with a mule and sent him for horses.

Returning to the car he cut a tent into strips to place beneath the wheels. The crew tore up shirts for the same purpose but still the car could not be driven out. Food and water ran low. The horses did not come. Then a wind sprang up and swept the loose sand away. The de Dion restarted, and set out again on the rutted trails.

On March 24th 1908 the Thomas passed through San Francisco after making the 3,800-mile east-west transcontinental journey in forty days. It turned north for Alaska en route for Asia via the Bering Strait.

No automobile had ever entered this wild territory before; the race was becoming an expedition. Alaska boasted no roads, no tracks; the cars had only rough sled trails to follow. Then the spring thaws began, and they were finally beaten.

In order to continue the race, the organisers altered the route. The cars were permitted to cross the Pacific by ship to Yokohama, drive across Japan, and take another ship to Vladivostock, in Russia.

The Thomas was credited with 15 days because of the time it had lost going into Alaska, and the Protos was penalised by 15 days because it had been put on a train from Pocatello, Idaho, to Seattle. Count de Dion in Paris withdrew his car, leaving only the Thomas and the Zust in the running for first place.

In Russia the racers found knee-deep floods. They took to the Trans-Siberian railway line and drove along it 500 miles to Harbin. Meanwhile, the Zust was suffering more misadventures: it caught fire, it frightened a horse which knocked down a boy, and its crew were suspected of spying.

At Tomsk, two teeth of the Thomas's driving gear broke and

Enormous crowds swarm round the Protos as it passes through Berlin.

repairs took four days, allowing the Protos to take the lead—although its penalty gave the others time in hand. Through Germany, between Berlin and Hanover, the Thomas and the Protos passed and re-passed each other as breakdown followed breakdown.

Finally Paris was reached. First car in was the Protos, but this was meaningless in view of the bonus and penalty marks. Four days later, on July 30th, the Thomas came in, to win with a time of 168 days, or five and a half months. Weeks later the Zust rattled into Paris.

The Thomas 'Flyer' was shipped back to the United States in triumph. It took part in a celebration procession through Broadway, with its torn and muddy Stars and Stripes (they had been flown all through the race) still aloft.

The Italian Zust was to suffer a final misfortune. It was brought over to England for exhibition, and while a mechanic was filling the tank with petrol it went up in a funeral pyre of flames.

The world's toughest, most adventurous race was over.

End of a giant. The burnt-out Zust in Britain.

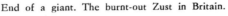

Renault, 1910.

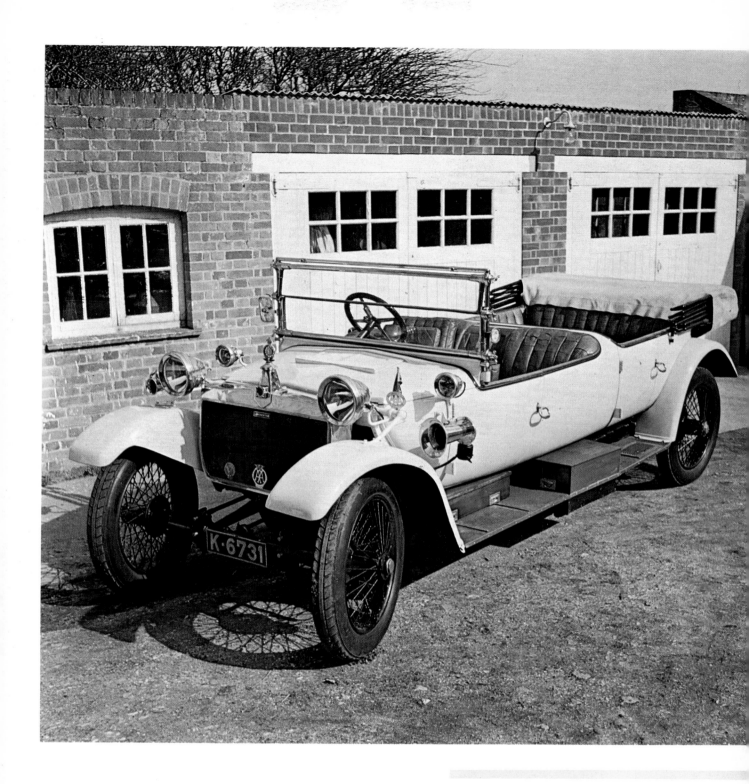

Lanchester, 1913: 38 h.p. six cylinder engine.

12 h.p. 1903 Lanchester.

A 1914 Dennis fire engine.

As the nineteenth century faded, and the motor car secured a foothold in the daily life of the civilised world, an increasing number of men of foresight and enterprise turned their eyes and their energies towards establishing a motor industry.

Many were the brave attempts to build a more efficient, more economical, safer, faster car. Many were the failures. Steam cars, gas cars, electric cars, they were all tried. Some were starkly dangerous—a naked flame within half a dozen yards would hazard the whole neighbourhood—some were as complicated to drive as a theatre organ, others, particularly the steamers, were actually quite efficient. However, these bizarre methods of propulsion slowly gave way to what, even in the early 1900s, was the well-tried petroleum spirit engine.

Dozens of different marques appeared during the early part of this century; names like the Pieper of Belgium, Vallée of France, Duryea of the United States, Standard of Britain, and Durkopp of Germany; names that in some cases lasted no longer than a few years, while others are still being produced in their millions today.

This chapter cannot hope to detail a hundredth part of the story of the great marques of motoring. Rather, a representative few have been briefly outlined; a selection that includes the King of Cars, the Rolls Royce, and the humble, reliable, everyday Austin. Some of the names that are here have long disappeared from the sales lists and the shows, some are still with us . . .

Austin

If farmer's son Herbert Austin (later Lord Austin) has produced nothing else, he would always have been remembered for his Austin Seven car, the diminutive vehicle that was the most successful of British cars, the car that made motoring possible for the many.

As a boy Austin went to Australia with an uncle, and worked there for the Wolseley Sheep Shearing Machine Company. When he came home to England in 1893, owning a share of the company, he became interested in motor cars, and eventually built one in the factory of his company in the Midlands.

A 1903 Wolseley.

123

Herbert Austin's first Longbridge car, about 1906. Austin is at the wheel.

His first car was a twin-cylinder, two-horsepower, built of steel tubing—a near copy of Bollée's three-wheeler.

A year or two later, in 1896, he built a second three-wheeler which he drove the 250 miles from Birmingham to Rhyl and back to prove its merit as a road vehicle. He produced his first four-wheeled car in 1899, and a year later entered it in the famous 1,000 miles trial organised by the Automobile Club, when it proved to be an outstandingly sturdy car.

A few years later the Wolseley Company was turning out 10 h.p. two-cylinder cars in quantity, and were the largest firm in Britain devoted to producing cars alone.

In 1905 Herbert Austin began to make cars under his own name at Longbridge, the first being the 25/30. Soon he was making cars of a half-dozen different horsepowers.

His crowning achievement, the Austin Seven, was first made in 1921. It made its début at Shelsley Walsh Hill climb, the smallest car to have been seen in Britain.

It was, in fact, a scaled-down version of a big car, housing a 747 c.c. engine producing 10½ b.h.p. at 2,500 r.p.m., and was capable of about 50 m.p.h.

It weighed only 8½ cwt and had brakes on all four wheels—some-

An early Austin landaulet.

An Austin Vitesse Phaeton, 1914.

thing new in light car design. It had faults. The brakes and steering were not all they might have been, and the clutch was vicious, but it was a wonderfully reliable little car. It was constructed with extremely strong members, it was cheap (£125), it was economical to run, and it was readily adapted for competition motoring.

By 1929 some 100,000 Sevens had been sold and the tiny car continued to be made, little altered, until 1938, by which time nearly 300,000 had been produced. A testimony to the strength and ruggedness of this simple vehicle is the fact that there are still thousands on the road today—and they are still in demand for competition work.

Crowning achievement, a 1922 Austin Seven.

Bugatti   Ettore Bugatti came of an artistic family, and many regard his cars as both aesthetical and mechanical works of art. Son of a painter and sculptor, Bugatti, born in Milan, studied sculpture for a time, but later turned to engineering.

He designed and built his first car, a three-wheeler, in 1898 when he was only 17, and followed it with another which boasted four engines, two in front of the driver and two at the rear of the car.

After he had shown a car at a Milan exhibition in 1901, and had won a cup and a medal, Baron de Dietrich commissioned Bugatti to design for his firm. Although still not 21, Bugatti accepted the offer and also began to design for a number of other motor manufacturers.

A 2.3 litre supercharged Bugatti.

In 1909 he set up his own works at Molsheim, near Strasbourg, and commenced to build cars that were years ahead of their time in design and mechanics. A series of racing and sports cars with superb steering and gear boxes and high performance soon made the name Bugatti revered in motor sport circles.

He also made, in 1927, the enormous Bugatti Royale, as long as a bus and with a 12,760 c.c. engine that was later developed for use in French railcars. Bugatti made the first of these for his own use; only a few were produced, mainly for royalty.

Cleanliness of line and superb mechanics were the watchwords of Bugatti's cars. And cleanliness was a byword in his factory; no tool was ever left dirty or out of place, nothing was allowed to spoil the pristine conditions in which his famous cars were made. Ettore Bugatti applied the same stern principles to himself as he did to his employees, all of whom he knew by name, despite the rapid expansion of his firm. His brilliant work had become a legend before he died in 1949.

Frenchman Alexandre Darracq was one of the first to make cars in great numbers. A one-time draughtsman, he began as a bicycle manufacturer, selling out his business in 1896 to become a wealthy man. Then he bought the Bollée four-wheel car patents and moved into the motor industry.

His first successful model was a small, single-cylinder voiturette, but the car for which he is best known today, is, of course, the 1904 12 h.p., two-cylinder model driven by John Gregson in the film *Genevieve*.

Darracq made 8 h.p. single- and 10 h.p. twin-cylinder taxi cabs that were used extensively in London and Paris, and later opened a factory near Naples to build them for Italy. However, there were problems about manufacturing in Italy, and Darracq sold his Italian interests in 1909 to a group who called themselves the 'Società Anonima Lombarda Fabbrica Automobili' or A.L.F.A. From this grew the Alfa-Romeo firm.

At the same time in France the Darracq firm was merged with Talbot, and Alexandre Darracq soon retired, a millionaire.

Darracq

To Frederick Lanchester, a great British engineer, goes the credit for building England's first really successful four-wheel car.

After a brief spell as a draughtsman, Lanchester joined a firm of gas engine manufacturers in Birmingham, where he designed a new unit and patented a number of improvements to existing gas engines.

In 1893, aged 25, he resigned in order to carry out experimental work. One of the first results was a petrol engine which he put into a boat: it was England's first motor boat.

Excited by the possibilities of petrol-engined transport, he went to Germany and Italy, looked over their cars and came home to build his own. Lanchester considered that Continental cars were handicapped by their direct derivation from carriages and bicycles. He intended to build his own car from first principles, uninfluenced by others. This he did. The car was completed in 1895, powered by an air-cooled, 5 h.p. single-cylinder engine.

Lanchester later redesigned it as an 8 h.p. twin, and in 1898 built a second car which won him a gold medal for design and performance at the Richmond Motor Show.

He made a third car—and a fourth—which split into two parts during the 1,000 Miles Trial of 1900, a hefty reporter who was occupying the rear seat being left in the road—with the unpowered half!

Frederick Lanchester began commercial production in 1901 with a 10 h.p. car, offered in either water or air-cooled form, and production continued under his direction for four years.

In 1909 Lanchester became a consultant to Daimler's, leaving his brothers George and Frank to carry on the motor business.

Later in life he found a new interest, research into aerodynamics.

Lanchester

127

Morris William Morris gave Britain its first mass-produced car. The story of how the humble bicycle agent rose to become Lord Nuffield, one of Britain's greatest philanthropists, has been told many times: it is one of the greatest success stories of the century.

The first Morris Oxford.

He started as a cycle agent in Oxford at the age of 16 with £4 capital, moved on to motor cycles and built his first car in 1912. It was called the Morris Oxford, and sold at the low price of £165.

In America, Ford was showing what could be done with mass production in the car industry. William Morris laid plans to mass produce a middle-class family car. It was to be the Morris Cowley. The car with the famous bull-nosed radiator was planned in 1915, but it was 1919 before production could start, mainly because of the difficulty Morris had in getting engines.

He wanted 5,000 for the first year and had to go to America for them. The car was introduced at £465, then, as costs fell and sales rose, Morris followed Ford's example and cut the price. Three cuts brought it down to £255 and the foundations had been laid for one of Britain's biggest industrial concerns.

. . . and the famous Bullnose Oxford of the 'twenties.

Napier The elegant Napier was the first successful six-cylinder car. Its story began when S. F. Edge bought the 8 h.p. twin-cylinder Panhard-Levassor, the car that had come second in the Paris-Marseilles-Paris race of 1896.

Edge decided to have its tiller steering altered to wheel steering, pneumatic tyres in place of solid ones, and a radiator fitted. He gave the job to Montague Napier, a friend whose family firm made weighing machines. Napier became intensely interested in the conversion, and designed a new engine to replace the Panhard one.

Edge was impressed with the result, formed a company, and ordered

A Gordon Bennett Napier during the eliminating trials of 1904.

a number of twin- and four-cylinder cars. By 1900, due largely to these first orders, Napier was in business in the motor car industry.

The four-cylinder (16 h.p.) car was very fast. Edge and C. S. Rolls drove it in the Paris-Toulouse race of 1900 where it ran well until an ignition failure put it out of the running.

The following year Napier designed a 16-litre, four-cylinder monster which weighed some three and a half tons. This, too, was a failure. The next year he decided to apply different principles to his design, and produced an ultra-light 6½-litre car in which Edge won the 1902 Gordon Bennett race.

Montague Napier built a works at Acton Vale and there produced his first six-cylinder car in 1904. Other people had produced six-cylinder cars before, but they had been failures. This one was a success and opened up a new realm of luxury travel—six-cylinder motoring.

One such six-cylinder car was used by Arthur Macdonald to push the world land speed record up to 104.65 m.p.h. in 1905. Edge also broke many records in a Napier.

When Edge left the firm in 1912, Napiers lost their chief publicist and salesman. Napier cars ceased to be made in 1925, but the name was not lost to the world of mechanics, for the firm switched to making aircraft engines.

A 1909 30 h.p. Napier.

Two Veteran Napiers on the London to Brighton Run. *Left:* a 1907 car. *Right:* the 1900 model.

A two seater Renault of 1909.

Louis Renault was the draughtsman son of a well-to-do Paris draper. In 1897, when he was 20, he bought a $1\frac{3}{4}$-h.p. de Dion Bouton tricycle and was soon planning a more efficient vehicle.

Around the de Dion engine he designed a car, lighter than virtually any on the road. He took his brothers, Marcel and Fernand into partnership and started production.

In their first year as a company they made six cars; after Renault had taken the first two places in the Paris-Trouville race of 1899, the figure shot up to 350 a year.

In 1902 the Renaults began to make their own engines instead of relying on the de Dion ones. The resourceful Louis knew the value

A tall, 1914, $4\frac{1}{2}$-litre Renault at Silverstone.

of racing to demonstrate his lightweight cars: he entered them in many sporting events. In the Paris-Vienna race of 1902 a Mors skidded badly and broke a wheel of Louis' car. Louis found some hedge-row wood, cut out spokes, repaired the wheel and carried on.

In 1906 a Renault won the French Grand Prix—the finest publicity in the world for a car at that time. Between 1908 and the First World War the popularity of the marque was great and a great number of two-cylinder Renaults were imported to Britain.

The largest car that Renaults made in quantity in the Vintage period was the big six-cylinder, nine-litre '45' which was produced until 1928.

Rolls-Royce

From the 1905 Rolls-Royce catalogue.

Henry Royce, son of a miller, was a crane engineer living in Manchester when he bought a French car at the turn of the century. He was appalled by its crudity. 'I could build a better one myself,' he said. And Royce was no pipe-dreamer: he set out to do so.

In 1904 he drove the first Royce car out of his workshop. It was a two-cylinder 10 h.p. car and the remarkable thing about it was that it was almost silent.

In London the Honourable Charles Rolls was told about the car. Rolls came of a very different background from Royce, who had sold newspapers at the age of nine, after his father's death. Rolls was the son of Lord Llangattock; he had a town house, a country seat and an ocean-going yacht. He also had a business selling Panhard and Minerva cars.

Rolls asked Royce to come and see him. But he was told that it would be impossible to get Royce away from his work-bench. So

A three-cylinder Rolls-Royce tonneau built in 1905-6.

131

The original Silver Ghost, 1906-7 . . .

Rolls went north to see Royce, had a demonstration drive in the car, and recognised that it was far superior to the cars that he was selling. A world-famous partnership began.

Royce made the cars: Rolls raced and sold them. The power was raised to 15 h.p. from three cylinders, then later to 20 h.p. powered by four cylinders.

In 1906 the firm decided to concentrate on a one-model policy. The model was the Silver Ghost, a six-cylinder, seven-litre-engined car incorporating the new classic Rolls-Royce radiator. Charles Rolls launched it with a superb advertising campaign.

The longest non-stop reliability test any car had undergone up to that time was 7,000-odd miles. The Silver Ghost was to run 15,000 miles non-stop—up and down from London to Scotland until the distance was covered. And it did.

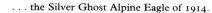

. . . the Silver Ghost Alpine Eagle of 1914.

The Silver Ghost continued with few alterations for 19 years (before being superseded by the Phantom) and established the name Rolls-Royce as synonymous with the best in workmanship, with perfection in mechanics and with the greatest car in the world.

Tragedy broke up the partnership in 1910 when Rolls, a pioneer aviator, crashed in his Wright biplane. Royce, 14 years older, lived on until 1933 and was knighted before his death for his great contribution to the industry.

Vauxhall

Alexander Wilson, a young Scots engineer, began making marine engines for London's river tugs in 1857. He called his Wandsworth Road factory the Vauxhall Ironworks.

In 1903 the Vauxhall Ironworks produced their first small motor car, a single-cylinder, tiller-steered, two-seater.

The simplicity of these first models, their low price, and their comparative reliability endeared them to the public, and during the following year a Mark II was produced for 130 guineas. It was similar to the original model but had the added luxury of a detachable seat which when in use accommodated a passenger in a precarious position on top of the bonnet. Owners took it for granted that the company would be closely interested in their product's performance. Letters such as the following poured into the Ironworks:

August 4th 1903

Dear Sirs,

You will be wondering how I got along with my little Car. Well, she acted like a charm all the way, and never refused duty at any time, taking the hills like level ground. I may tell you that I took her across London Bridge on Saturday morning and drove all through Borough Market, where the traffic kept two policemen as busy as they could be. After that exploit I don't fear any traffic, although I still prefer open country . . .

One can imagine the confusion if today's countless millions of car owners wrote in to the manufacturers telling of their traffic exploits!

The Vauxhall Company moved to their present site in Luton, Bedfordshire, in 1905 when they were joined by designer Laurence Pomeroy Senior, who began to plan the 'middle-class' cars that were to win so many successes at Brooklands.

In 1911 Pomeroy designed the famous Prince Henry, after the Prinz-Heinrich Trials of Germany. This highly successful four-cylinder sports car took Vauxhalls into the prize-winning class and proved to be one of the best advertisements of all time for both the company and its designer.

For hill climbing, Pomeroy modified a Prince Henry, and it was entered in the Shelsley Walsh event of 1913. It broke all records and became part of the legend of motor sport under its new name, the Vauxhall 30/98.

1903. The first Vauxhall.

1904. Mark 2.

1905. Vauxhall moves to Luton.

1905. A steering wheel takes over from the tiller.

1906. The first model with the familiar fluted bonnet.

1908. A Vauxhall two seater tourer.

1909. Another smart two seater.

1911. The Prince Henry.

1912-13. Prince Henry with special racing body.

1916. Staff car.

1919-26. The classic 30/98.

A parade of Vauxhalls.

the motor car in world war I

In their rush to praise the rôle of the tank in the First World War, historians have given scant thanks to the part the automobile played in the conflict. Yet the plain touring car was the first military automobile and was used in local wars in Mexico long before 1914. The Mexicans simply adapted one of the passenger seats to act as a base for their machine gun.

The British Pennington Fighting Autocar of 1896 was one of the first attempts to armour the automobile and is therefore looked on as the forerunner of the tank.

And when action started in 1914, the allies realised that though tanks were very good at crossing 'impossible' terrain and mowing down the enemy, they couldn't carry supplies or move troops in a war which was being run on a much faster scale than had been known before. Enter the unarmoured car—the 'soft' vehicle.

General Sir A. Currie's Rolls-Royce outside Headquarters at Hersin Company, 23rd August 1917.

A Rolls-Royce light armoured car. Abbeville, May 1916.

Battle of Arras. Troops boarding buses in Arras to go back for a rest, May 1917.

Scene on a road near Peronne during the Retreat. Military vehicles loaded with troops, staff cars, and refugees with carts and cattle fill the road. March 1918.

Captain MacIntyre, M.C., of the 7th Light Car Patrol left our lines at 10 a.m. on 23rd October 1918, in a Ford car and under a white flag, with a letter demanding the surrender of Aleppo.

An experimental Light 'D' tank. Experimental tracks fitted to Overland chassis.

With the backing of the Government, the R.A.C. put a notice in *The Times*. It read:

'*August 5th, 1914.*
'*An Appeal to Motorists.*
'*The Royal Automobile Club will be glad to receive the names of members and associates who will offer the services of their cars or their services with their cars either for home or foreign service, in case of need.*
'*It is requested that the make and horsepower of the car should be stated.*'

The response was excellent and the Scottish Autocar industry quickly collected 1,100 vehicles and 1,000 civilian drivers. Of the thousands of cars that came into the army's hands, the majority were used for general transport with only slight adaptation. Other, more sturdy cars were converted into armoured cars, and many beautiful Rolls-Royces suffered this ignominious change.

The Ford car made a greater name for itself in the First World War for its reliablity, and Ford convoys could often be seen, not only in Europe but also in the Middle East. Taxis were particularly welcomed by the Transport Divisions; a fact which left such a dearth of them in London that the impossibility of finding a taxi became a popular theme with the *Punch* cartoonists.

The open-topped double-decker bus was used widely, and many

An Austin armoured car. (1914-1918 War.)

soldiers can remember their rides to and from the front lines in these trundling bone-breakers that had known a much more peaceful service.

And when the fighting had stopped and the troops returned to their homes, many of these vehicles went back with them to carry on their work in peacetime. It says much for the makers of those 'fighting' motor cars.

A Ford convoy on the Jabel Hamrin.

Vauxhall elegance: a 1923 30/98.

working models

The life of a Vintage car is often a tough one. For unlike their older brothers they are usually working cars. Veterans are, after all, museum pieces and must be treated with the caution and care such items demand.

Not that care is not lavished on Vintage vehicles; but these cars of the 'twenties are actually allowed to get dirty now and then! An owner who uses his vintage transport to take him to and from the office obviously cannot keep spokes, mudguards, and the underside of his car looking as though it has just rolled off the production line.

Vintage Day at Silverstone.

At the start of a vintage race at Silverstone.

There are a great number of rallies, races, speed tests, and driving tests held every year for members of the Vintage Sports Car Club, but the highlight of each season is the gathering of the fans at Silverstone, usually during April.

Here these hardy vehicles show their paces. There is a Vintage sports car race, a Grand Prix open to Vintage racing cars, and an Edwardian race, high-speed trials and so on . . .

The lap times are a surprise to the newcomer. Even the 1908 Itala (after which the G.P. race is named) sometimes gets around the Club Circuit at over 60 m.p.h. and the sports cars lap in the seventies . . .

A 1914 Sunbeam waits for the flag to start a high-speed trial.

Below left : a Riley Special, 1929 vintage, corners at speed . . .

. . . *and below right :* a 1924 Hispano-Suiza fights through the same corner at Silverstone.

A 1910 ten-litre Fiat on the grid before the Itala Trophy race.

Smooth driving in a 1926 Amilcar . . .

. . . and an exciting moment as two 1921 Bentleys chase into a sharp bend on the Club Circuit.

Accepted thoroughbred. A 1931 Alfa Romeo.

Rugged simplicity. *Left:* The wheel of a Vintage Grand Prix Maserati. *Above:* The front end of a Lagonda. The lamps are turned to prevent damage from stones flying up from the road.

Tight fit. Bentley power unit.

Duel in the sun. A 1926 Amilcar passes the 1914 Sunbeam.

A 1925 Sunbeam backs into line at Silverstone.

143

warning glory

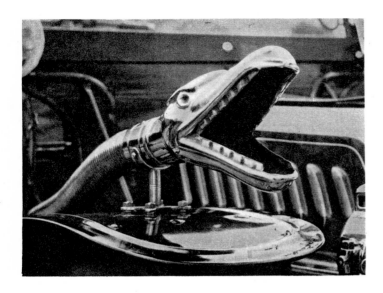

You can almost hear the clarion call of the post-horn. The graceful volutes hint at regal fanfares, and compared to the functional electric klaxons even the bicycle squeaker is imperious . . . The snake speaks for itself . . .

bentley
years
at
le mans

After the First World War W. O. Bentley, sportsman, engineer, motor car agent, decided to design and build his own vehicles.

Inspired partly by the successful Mercedes and partly by the fast Peugeot three-litre racer, the Bentley was well ahead of its time. With a cruising speed of about 65 m.p.h. the car, large and heavy though it was, could travel at some 30 miles to the gallon—an uncommon feat in the days of petrol-thirsty power units.

Just five years after he had made his first experimental car, one of his products made history at Le Mans, the great French circuit that was even then running its annual 'Grand Prix d'Endurance'. A privately entered Bentley won against heavy, sponsored opposition.

Encouraged by this win W. O. Bentley entered his own team the following year. Bad fortune dogged his cars, and they all retired before the end of the race due to annoyingly trivial faults.

They were out of luck again in 1926, but in 1927 they took part in (and won) one of the most dramatic, the most extraordinary events Le Mans has ever seen. The next year a Bentley took the chequered flag again ... in 1929 the works team sailed home with a 1—2—3—4 win, the greatest British victory in the history of motor racing up to that time.

1930 brought W. O. his fourth magnificent win at Le Mans. It is sad to reflect that in Bentley's case the publicity from the victories won on the circuits of Europe did not prevent his company taking the road to financial failure—and eventual liquidation.

But let us bring to life the episode which was perhaps the sporting climax of those vintage days at Le Mans, a climax so inspiring that the late 'twenties have come to be known to motoring enthusiasts as 'The Bentley Years' ...

The start of the 1927 race at Le Mans. The three Bentleys are first away.

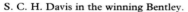

S. C. H. Davis in the winning Bentley.

The race-course commentator takes over ...

'Good evening and welcome to Le Mans, 1927. At the moment there's high drama here. No cars have appeared for some minutes and no one seems to know what has happened.

'Twenty-two cars set out this afternoon on the twenty-four-hour Grand Prix d'Endurance and the three British Bentleys were first away. They were still leading when the cars last came through in the dusk with six hours gone.

'A Bentley won this testing race for the first and only time in 1924 and today W. O. Bentley is set on a sweeping victory. His team consists of two of the familiar three-litre cars and a new four-and-half-litre model, almost identical to the three-litres except for the cylinder block.

'It was the four-and-half-litre—car number one in the race—that was first away, driven by Frank Clement, the Bentley test driver, followed by the cars of Dr Dudley Benjafield, the Harley Street consultant, and Baron d'Erlanger, the banker.

'And now as night closes in the only threat to them seems to be the Aries of Chassagne and Laly.

'With 200-odd miles covered the drivers changed over, L. G. Callingham, who is making his début with Bentley, taking over the four-and-half-litre, Sammy Davis taking over from Dr Benjy, and George Duller, also well known as a horse trainer, relieving d'Erlanger.

'The daylight faded, the cars' lamps were switched on and the illuminations came on all round the circuit, but the Bentleys have gone thundering on, announcing their coming to their pits by code-blasts on their horns, one for the four-and-half-litre, two for the Duller-d'Erlanger car and three for the Davis-Benjafield. And that was the order when they last passed through . . .

'But now they are overdue. There is no sound of the engines and W. O. is looking anxiously from the three stop-watches in the pits to the track and back.

'What is happening out there? Where are they?

'Wait . . . I can hear an engine at last. Yes, a car is coming, one car on its own, going slowly. I still can't see it. It's got no lights. Which is it? Now I can see it in the light of the pits. It's the No. 3 Bentley driven by Sammy Davis . . . but what a state it's in. One front wing is twisted back over the bonnet, a wheel is wobbling. Davis is out of the car and jacking up the front end. We'll find out what has happened in a second . . .

Dr Benjafield (No. 3) overtakes Chantrel's Schneider.

'The news is bad. There has been a multiple pile-up at the White House corner. A French Schneider spun and crashed, blocking half the road. Callingham came round and saw it too late—it's a blind corner of course—and in trying to avoid the Schneider he swerved into a ditch and the four-and-half-litre Bentley turned over, blocking the rest of the road.

'George Duller's Bentley went into the four-and-half-litre and climbed on top of it. throwing Duller over a hedge. Then Davis arrived and skidded sideways into the other two Bentleys. Another car has crashed behind them.

'Fortunately there seem to have been no serious injuries. Tabourin, who was driving the Schneider, is thought to have broken ribs. Duller has been cut about the face but has gone back down the track to warn other drivers. Callingham and Davis are unhurt. But the number three Bentley is the only car involved in the crash that is still able to run, and I don't know whether it is capable of running any further. What a blow to W.O.'s hopes.

'Davis has put a new wheel on now. He has changed the lamp bulbs and done some wiring and taping. Now all the lights are on except for the offside headlamp. He has strapped the battery back on the running board—it was hanging off like a broken limb when he came in. And he is beating the mudguard back to something like its proper place. W.O. is trying to check that axle; it looks as though it is bent. Davis is saying that it is fit to drive. But can it last another eighteen hours?

'Davis is getting back in the car. He is going to continue the race! Officials have pulled the cars off the track at the White House and the road is reasonably clear again but the Aries has already gone through. It seems that Davis has a pretty forlorn hope of winning—or even lasting the course. But there he goes! That Bentley engine sounds healthy but he has no offside headlamp; the front axle—and indeed the frame of the car, must be suspect after that crash.

'Davis is away, taking it fairly steady but considerably faster than most of us would care to risk. The Aries is well in the lead now. And

The multiple crash at White House Corner. Davis's Bentley skids into the other cars. (Courtesy *The Autocar*.)

Le Mans, 1928. Birkin's Bentley at Arnage Turn. (Courtesy *The Autocar.*)

it is starting to rain. Here is Davis round again. The rain is quite heavy now. He is wearing a talc face screen of the type sold for lady motorists, as a kind of visor: I gather he thinks this is better than goggles in the wet.

'Davis is going faster now—and sounding healthy—but it does not seem possible that the Bentley can ever hope to catch the Aries which is moving very well indeed. Now one of Davis's side lights has gone and he has fixed a police lantern in its place. He hands over to Dr Benjafield . . .

'The Bentley keeps coming into the pits for pieces to be tied up, yet it is still going. Davis and Benjafield are doing marvels. I never expected to see a car in this condition among the leaders at Le Mans. It's dawn now and the Bentley is still there.

'Four hours to go now and the Aries is over 40 miles ahead of the Bentley. If anything happens to the opposition the Bentley can still win but it seems an extremely faint chance. But what's this? W. O. Bentley is putting out a signal for Benjy to go faster. Surely the doctor is already driving right on the limit for such a crippled car!

'But, no, Benjafield is beginning to narrow the gap. He is gaining on the Aries. It's only 30 miles ahead now. Twenty . . . fifteen . . . ten. And yes, the Aries is making an odd noise. I think the cam shaft drive is going. W.O. must have spotted it early. He's trying to make the Aries crack.

'The Aries team have realised what is happening at last. Laly drives in to the pits and Jean Chassagne is taking over. He is stepping up the pace . . . he is increasing the lead again but the noise is getting worse. Dr Benjafield in the Bentley is going faster still. One of these cars has got to crack? Which will it be?

'Here's the answer. The No. 3 Bentley has just come through again but there is no sign of the Aries. The Aries has stopped. W.O.'s gamble has come off. Now it only remains to see if the Bentley can last out to the finish. Here it comes again. It's coming in to the pits, one of the mudguards hanging off. They are strapping it on and now it's out again and, incredibly, it still sounds healthy . . . Now it is in again and Benjafield is handing over to Sammy Davis for the last laps.

'There are only eight cars left in the race now. No one here would have thought the Bentley would be among them. But here comes the British car on the last lap. Davis is crossing the line now and the Bentley has won the 1927 Le Mans with Salmson cars second and third. And what a race it has been . . .'

A 1903 de Dion Bouton in the London to Brighton run.

A 1928 Salmson at speed during a Vintage event.

Riley at work, 1930.

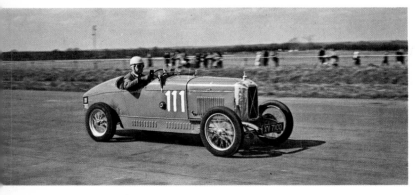

Above : Invicta at rest, 1931.

Left : Vintage greyhound, 1934. The fast Derby-Maserati.

Above : A 1914 Mercedes.

Below : A 'Brecia' Bugatti, Vintage 1922 (1496 cc).

the men at the wheel

Since motor sport first began there have been men who have devoted their energies, their time, and their money to the competitive events. They are the men whose names stand out strongly in the story of this tough, hazardous sport, men whose names are synonymous with speed, with courage, and with all that is colourful in racing. This breed has continued unbroken from the time of Levassor, to Hill and Clark in the present day. Here are a few brief cameos of some of the great drivers of the Heroic Days of motor racing, the Veteran and Vintage Era . . .

Selwyn Francis Edge.

Puncture! The Napier slewed to a halt. Out leapt driver and mechanic Selwyn Francis Edge and his cousin, Cecil Edge.

They burrowed in the car for their tools. They had all disappeared, somehow lost in crossing the snow-covered Arlberg Pass into Germany.

S. F. Edge was shocked but unbeaten. This was a race—the 1902 Gordon Bennett Cup Race from Paris to Innsbruck—and he was lying second. Bare-handed he attacked the tyre cover, ripping it from the rim, heedless of broken nails and bruised fingers.

Three punctures later the Edges' fingers were raw, torn and bleeding. But S.F. continued his pursuit of the leading car, the Panhard of the Chevalier de Knyff, until the French car finally broke down.

The Napier entered Innsbruck the winner; Edge had scored Britain's first-ever motor racing victory, for until this moment Continental cars and drivers had been unassailable.

Edge, who raced to gain publicity for Napier cars, in which he had an interest, was Britain's first motor racing hero . . .

While Edge was wrestling with punctures in Germany another British driver was fighting troubles of a different sort on the same road. He was Charles Jarrott, Panhard's manager in England, who was driving one of the firm's cars in the Paris-Vienna race which ran concurrently with the Gordon Bennett event as far as Innsbruck.

Jarrott's troubles began on the second day out from Paris. With nearly 400 miles to go, the frame of his car fractured. The cars were sealed each night and could not be touched but, as soon as the Panhard was released in the morning, Jarrott's mechanic was sent off to buy some bolts while Jarrott took the legs off a hotel table.

The start of a Vintage race at Silverstone.

Charles Jarrott in his Panhard during the
Paris-Vienna race of 1902.

With them he built a stiffener to hold the car frame together and
rejoined the race. Then the cooling system began to leak. Solder was
applied, but new leaks occurred and, for a time, the unfortunate
mechanic was obliged to lie prone on the Panhard's bonnet, holding
a towel round the leak, the exhaust pipe painfully blistering his hands,
while Jarrott drove on.

Brakes burned out, the steering developed a fault and, near Vienna,
the gearbox broke.

Jarrott borrowed a bicycle and rode back in search of help but
found only a policeman, whom he accidentally ran down. He narrow-
ly avoided arrest. Returning to the car he continued driving on the one
remaining gear. The clutch could not be withdrawn, but spectators
push-started the Panhard and, in first gear, it rattled on towards the
finish. With the silencer and other parts falling off and leaving a trail
of litter to mark its progress, the Panhard limped across the line and
then stopped for good.

Jarrott, later to play a big part in the founding of the A.A., had
finished second—with only two-thirds of the car—and an average
speed of 41.1 m.p.h.!

Artist's impression of Jarrott and the Panhard at the Circuit des Ardennes.
(Courtesy *The Autocar*.)

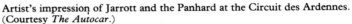

It was soon after this that Sir Algernon Lee Guinness acquired an
eight-cylinder 200 h.p. Darracq. With his younger brother, Kenelm
Lee Guinness, as his mechanic, he would drive to a quiet, straight
Surrey road and mark out white lines a kilometre apart.

Then, while friends blocked off the road and watched for the village
policeman, Algy and Kenelm roared over the measured stretch.

Algy became a wild, fast, hair-raising-to-watch driver; he thrilled
spectators of the 1906 T.T. by the way he hurled his car round the
Isle of Man's mountain circuit to finish second.

Kenelm, known as Bill, developed into a more serious, calculating
driver. In a white, knitted cap he drove for many years in the French
Grand Prix as Sunbeam's No. 1 pilot.

Henry Segrave was yet another great Sunbeam driver. As a comparative unknown he was driving an Opel at Brooklands when a tyre burst. Brilliantly he held the car on its line, and continued without noticeable loss of speed. In the pits was Louis Coatalen, the Sunbeam designer, who saw the manoeuvre and determined to have this man on the Sunbeam side. Segrave joined the team to win the first major British race, the 1921 Brooklands 200-mile event. The same year he became the first British driver to win a French Grand Prix.

Sheer speed delighted Segrave—one of the first drivers to wear a crash helmet—and he turned to land speed record breaking, which won him a knighthood, the first such honour to be awarded for achievements in motor sport. He died tragically, attacking water speed records on Lake Windermere.

Then there was Woolf 'Babe' Barnato, the greatest of the Bentley Boys according to W. O. Bentley in his autobiography. Babe was the wealthy sportsman who financed the firm. An enthusiast of cricket, boxing and athletics, Barnato began motor racing in a medley of odd cars, then graduated to an enormous six and a half litre Bentley.

A virtuoso at the wheel, Barnato drove three times at Le Mans—and won every time. In 1928 he took the flag with a cracked frame and no water, in 1929 he led the Bentley procession in a Speed Six, and in 1930 he scored a hat trick which ended in his winning a battle between the Bentley and the great German driver Caracciola in a Mercedes-Benz.

Let us go back now to 1912, when a crazy-looking flying machine lurched from the roof of a little house in Italy and crashed to the ground to break up. From the wreckage its builder scrambled unhurt, as he was to emerge from many other crashes during his stormy lifetime.

His name was Tazio Nuvolari, born in Mantua (on the former Mille Miglia route) and known to his neighbours as 'The Mad One'. Soon after his flying fiasco he switched his attentions from air travel to motor cycling and then to cars.

Held by many to be the greatest driver of all time, he drove in utterly unorthodox style. Typical of his bold tactics was his driving in the Mille Miglia of 1930. Driving an Alfa-Romeo, he was unable to catch Achille Varzi's faster Maserati.

But the last part of the race finished in the dark. Nuvolari cut his lights and began to overhaul the unsuspecting Varzi, who had no idea that there was a car closing in behind him and had eased off.

With a few miles to go, Nuvolari switched on his lights, flashed past the startled Varzi and won. The motor racing spectators of his day considered Nuvolari to be almost superhuman. His reactions were so rapid that they thought he had the gift of clairvoyance into the near future. They would work out his chances in a race this way: if Tazio had a car equal to the best in the event, he would certainly win; if his car was 10 m.p.h. slower than the best he would certainly win; if his car was 20 m.p.h. slower than the best he would almost certainly win.

Tazio Nuvolari.

155

And such was the uncanny skill of the wiry little Italian that this type of forecasting usually worked!

Rudolf Caracciola was a driver of a different type: immaculate, cool, a copybook driver. Born in 1909 of German parentage, despite his Italian name, he began racing motor cycles in 1922. From this sport he learned the complex arts of balance and control, and he applied them with outstanding success to four-wheeled sport. His greatest victories came slightly after the Vintage era, but they were so spectacular that they merit him a place in the list of the truly 'greats'.

One of his most notable races was the 1930 Le Mans. The Bentleys were the main opposition—a team of six—to his big Mercedes. Birkin had been briefed to set a killing pace in his Bentley, and Barnato had been told to harass the German by overtaking him, and falling back, right through the race. Barnato won the race, but the lone Mercedes driven by Rudi Caracciola held on for hours despite failing electrical equipment, making the latter part of the event a wheel-to-wheel battle that thrilled the great crowds at the French circuit.

His record is one of the most impressive in the sport. In G.P. races from 1934 to 1939 he took no less than sixteen firsts, ten second places, and five third positions . . .

Rudolf Caracciola wins a Nurburgring event in 1927.

There were, of course, many great names during these formative days of motor racing. These were the years when competition was fierce in this new and exciting sport and, as always, the times produced the men. And what men they were; wild men or calculating ones, cool or firebrand, they all had the qualities that every racing driver needs: courage, dedication to their sport, the burning will to win—and that sixth sense that warns them of danger just a split second ahead of the ordinary man.

london to brighton in the 'sixties

How many of the multitude of spectators who flank the Brighton Road know what it's all about? One in a hundred—a thousand? And does it matter? Of course not. What *is* important is the fact that this annual trip brings pleasure to countless thousands of ordinary people and satisfaction to the participants.

The Brighton Run is arranged so that all the cars assemble at London's Hyde Park in the dawn hours of a Sunday morning, then set out at brief intervals to drive to Brighton where they assemble on the front for prize-giving and a short parade. It's as simple as that. But what happens—and what doesn't—on that journey makes the run such an attraction. For these vehicles, all about sixty years old, were built for a more leisurely form of motoring. Their brakes aren't what they should be for today's traffic, their suspension is cart-crude in many cases, and occasionally things happen to them which don't to modern cars!

Yet the drivers who assembled their cars along the Serpentine on this mild morning in November were nothing if not hopeful. Of course there would be plenty of breakdowns, but at least nothing would happen to *their* mounts—which had been so carefully prepared. The morning was dry and as the regular runners know, dry conditions make all the difference. Not for them the luxury of windscreens, roofs and side doors. For many, the only protection was the clothing they wore.

By half-light, the crowds were already milling around the cars. Owners were summing up their chances of a smooth trip, passengers were adding an extra blanket to their outfits and the public were making the most of what little light there was to photograph the more colourful of the entrants.

At 8 a.m. the first of the cars was away to a great cheer. The honour fell to a spindly 1896 Arnold. And so they set off at regular intervals. For the earlier makes, Brighton must have seemed a long way away.

Hyde Park at 7 a.m. on a Sunday morning in November. The cars are lined up for the start of the London-Brighton Run.

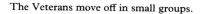

The Veterans move off in small groups.

157

This 1900 Benz arrived safely in Brighton, in spite of the alarming smoke trail.

A Benz, a Decauville and a Lutzmann pass the Palace.

American entry. Jack Frost's 1899 Haynes-Apperson Surrey.

From America, Jack Frost sent his 1899 Haynes-Apperson, an enormous vehicle with a flat twin engine. Its departure earned a special cheer, for although it was not the most attractive car on show, it was certainly one of the most unusual.

Of the original entry of 215, only 22 failed to start—which shows the amount of effort which was put into the preparation of these ancient cars. This figure included the unfortunate steam car belonging to Alec Hodson which blew up on the starting line. Eventually they were all away and steaming (some literally) over Westminster Bridge. It is here in previous years that the first signs of age have shown in some of the cars, and owners have found themselves underneath their ailing veterans almost within shouting distance of the start. Thanks to the cold weather (and the attendant lack of initial overheating), all made Westminster. But already the two main tasks for the drivers approached—those of keeping the passengers warm and the engines cool. At Waterloo came the first casualty, with J. S. Corry attacking his 1902 Benz with a screwdriver. Spectators in Brixton were also treated to some fine examples of running repairs and the now-familiar scene of passengers pushing the cars up the 'steep' gradients in that area.

The faster, 1903-4 models were soon speeding past the front markers but were often forced to stop on the way to maintain the average speed limits set by the R.A.C. This decision to limit the speed of the faster cars put a stop to the 'dices' which formed the unofficial highlights of some of the earlier runs.

Despite the heavy traffic from the modern motorists who followed the cavalcade all the way down to the coast, the police and R.A.C. did a competent job of control, and this, coupled with the public's knowledge of the braking limitations of the early cars, led to no serious accidents, though one owner was unfortunate enough to turn his precious model over into a hedge.

By the time the later starters had reached Bolney, the 1897 Benz of Sir Hugh Dawson had reached Brighton and was making its triumphal entry into Madeira Drive.

As they arrived the cars swung on to the front and into the reception centre where the Mayor of Brighton greeted them to the cheers of the tiered audience above the front.

The sixty fifth anniversary of 'Emancipation Day' was over.

A 1903 Darracq sweeps past a crowded gallery of spectators.

A de Dion Bouton of 1902 at Brighton.

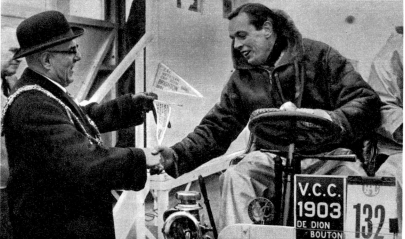

Mr P. H. Turvey receives his pennant from the Mayor.

Acknowledgements

The author and the publishers wish to thank the following for permission to reproduce photographs and other illustrations:
The Science Museum London, Mr R. B. Prosser,
Daimler-Benz of Germany, Mr D. R. Grossmark,
The Rank Organisation, The Veteran Car Club of Great Britain,
The Vintage Sports Car Club, The Ford Motor Company, U.S.A.,
Vauxhall Motors, The Veteran Motor Car Club of America,
Jaguar Cars Ltd, Wheeler-Roberts Writers Ltd,
The Royal Automobile Club, The Automobile Association,
The Montagu Museum, *Autocar, Motor Sport,*
Mr Anthony Davis, The Ford Motor Company, Dagenham,
The British Motor Corporation, Rolls-Royce Ltd, Harrods Ltd,
The Motor, The Imperial War Museum, Mr Kenneth Higgs,
The Veteran and Vintage Magazine, Autosport,
and *Punch* for numerous cartoons and research facilities.

Answers to Quiz
questions on page 38

1. The Mercedes car was named after Mercedes Jellinek, daughter of the Daimler representative in Nice.
2. An 1886 Danish-built Hammel from a Copenhagen museum. It has only one forward and one reverse gear and a top speed of 6 m.p.h.
3. (a) The Veteran Car Club of Great Britain was formed;
   (b) The Montagu Motor Museum opened at Beaulieu.
4. The Model T Ford. In 1917 it cost 360 dollars, equal to £73 10s.
5. A.1.
6. (a) Parry Thomas;
   (b) Tazio Nuvolari.
7. Brooklands, 1907.
8. Bumpers.
9. (a) Camille Jenatzy exceeded 60 m.p.h. in it;
   (b) Henry Ford exceeded 90 m.p.h. in it.
10. Founders of Lagonda, Hispano-Suiza and Cadillac respectively.
11. The Targa Florio races of Sicily.
12. Stenson Cooke of the A.A.
13. Fabrica Italiana d'Automobili Turin.
14. Passe-partout (after the valet in Jules Verne's *Around the World in 80 Days*).
15. The American White-Triplex of 1929.
16. The Rolls-Royce Silver Ghost, 1907-1926.
17. Bugatti Royale, type 41.
18. A 1905 Spyker.
19. Sir Henry O'Neill de Hane Segrave.
20. Rolls-Royce. He was Charles Rolls.
21. Parry Thomas's 'Babs'.